Exploring the
OLYMPIC
PENINSULA

Exploring the
OLYMPIC
PENINSULA

REVISED EDITION

By RUTH KIRK

SEATTLE: UNIVERSITY OF WASHINGTON PRESS

Published in cooperation with the
Olympic Natural History Association

PREFACE

On a map the Olympic Peninsula appears a mere thumb projecting from the upper corner of Washington, a jumping-off point west of Seattle and north of Olympia. Yet within it are wholly distinct realms: the bare rock and ice of the mountaintops; the flower meadows and tarns of the ridges; the lichen-upholstered trees in the rain forest; the quiet waterways inland, and the wild outer coast.

All of this can be sampled in a day or two, by car. But to *know* this peninsula takes a car, a truck, a horse, a boat, skis, climbing boots, an airplane—and a lifetime.

The frontier lingers here, and boots are as much everyday footgear as ladies' high heels or businessmen's oxfords. Rain forest ranchers pull on black Wellingtons without thought of the weather, and fishermen simply fold waders and hip boots to knee length to go ashore. Mountain climbers wear cleated boots and crampons with two-inch steel spikes that bite into the ice of glaciers. Loggers wear boots caulked with half-inch nails which are sure grip in the woods and sure ruin to floors (the reason signs on cafe doors and doctors' offices say, "Please, No Nails").

By definition, a peninsula must physically project from the mainland; this peninsula also projects scenically and culturally. Here "exploring" ranges from watching an Indian fashion a canoe from a cedar log, to scaling Mount Olympus; from mooching for salmon or stalking a cougar to photographing the rain forest.

This book is intended to help you take your pick and plan your time. Whatever strength it may have to guide wisely stems in large measure from resources beyond my own, as author. Persons too numerous to mention individually have joined me on road and trail, have furnished specialized knowledge, and have criticized the manuscript to correct at least its major flaws. The published references drawn upon are too many to be cited appropriately in a book of this sort, beyond a few of general interest. However, this does not imply a lack of awareness of my debt, for without the work and knowledge of others this volume would be impossible.

To all, my deep gratitude. And to the Olympic Peninsula itself, a special appreciation. No writer could ask for a land more filled with variety and enchantment.

RUTH KIRK

Port Angeles, Washington

CONTENTS

**Part 1
HISTORY**

INDIANS

Life on the Olympic Peninsula and all along the Northwest Coast was remarkably easy under primitive conditions. The Indians lived in houses built of wooden planks and traveled in canoes hollowed from cedar logs. Food needed only to be dug, caught, hunted, or harvested—clams, salmon, deer, berries, an unending supply and variety. Even the climate assured that nobody was hot for long in summer or menaced by cold in winter.

The Tribes: Nine main tribes inhabited the flat coastal land that rims the Peninsula. The Satsop, Wynoochee, and Humptulips tribes had villages along the rivers emptying into the Chehalis River, the present Olympia-to-Aberdeen region. The Copalis, Quinaielt, and Quileute tribes lived on the Pacific Coast. Their principal villages stood on the beach at the mouths of the best fishing rivers, but they also lived inland along the rivers. The Makahs were at Cape Flattery. The Clallams, the largest tribe on the Peninsula, were scattered along the Strait and south along Hood Canal as far as Seabeck. The Twanas, later called Skokomish after one of their villages, were concentrated at the lower end of Hood Canal.

Interspersed with the Clallams in the Port Townsend area were a few Chimacum Indians, often considered displaced Quileutes because of language similarities. The Hoh Indians, with a reservation of their own, belong to the Quileute tribe and have a joint chief with the LaPush Indians. The Queets Indians are part of the Quinaielt tribe and their village is on the Quinaielt Reservation. The Ozette Indians no longer exist as a separate group. Their village, midway between Neah Bay and LaPush, was Makah blended with Quileute.

Each tribe spoke a separate language, but they had much in common. They ate essentially the same foods, lived in the same sort of multifamily longhouses, even communed with the spirits in much the same way. They warred back and forth, and took one another as slaves; they intermarried, gave lavish gifts, and traded. The papers of a missionary on the Skokomish Reservation in the 1880's mention that his parishioners ate from dishes of mountain sheep horn made by the Stikine Indians, seven hundred miles north, warmed themselves in buffalo robes from the Klickitats and Yakimas, two hundred miles east, and stored trinkets in baskets from the Cowlitz, Chehalis, and Quinaielts, one hundred miles south and west.

The Quinaielts, even more than the other tribes, were traders because of their location on the coast. They traded clams and sea otter pelts from the

3

MAKAH DANCER

Copalis Indians to the Makahs for canoes and slaves; these in turn they traded as far as the Columbia River for guns and steel tools. The scale of values held two sea otter skins equivalent to one slave, one canoe, one gun, or fifteen to twenty blankets.

The mingling of Indian and white cultures began with the heyday of Hood Canal logging, 1870 to 1890, and it continued through the home-steading period that closed the century. Indians adopted white dress and tools, and white settlers depended on Indian dugouts for transportation. By the 1890's Quileute women had begun to boil water in iron pots instead of by dropping fire-heated stones into baskets, and Makahs had replaced their plaited cedar bark sails with canvas. By 1900 men at LaPush sold fish to white wholesalers even though they feared this might offend the Salmon People and cause them to come no more to the river.

Sea Hunters: Coast Indians prized whales above all. Makahs and Quil-eutes went to sea eight men in a canoe to hunt them. The weapons they pitted against the giants of the deep were harpoons made of elk bone and fastened to ropes twisted from cedar bark. If a harpooned whale headed oceanward instead of landward the men resigned themselves to tossing about for two or three days beyond sight of land. "Oh fine Whale," a harpooner chanted as he stood in the bow of a whaling canoe, "here is what you have been wanting. I give you my harpoon. Whale, you have it in your heart. Paddle now with your great flipper to the beach of my village."

Oil was the reason the whales were so highly prized. The resources of ocean and forest readily supplied protein and carbohydrate, but fat was comparatively scarce. When a hunting party returned towing a whale the whole village helped pull it high on the beach and watched while the blubber was cut in huge saddles and hung to drip. Rendering all of the oil often took a month.

Indians along the ocean coast of the Peninsula also welcomed the door-step delivery of one or two dead whales that washed ashore each winter. As recently as the 1930's Indians converged on Ruby Beach when word of a whale spread up and down the shore. It was a festive occasion—and a curious overlap of cultures as blubber dripped from the fenders and seats of Franklins and Model A's heading homeward to the reservations.

Fish and shellfish were the basic foods of all tribes on the Olympic Peninsula. Salmon choked the rivers: the year around, wave after wave of scaly hordes pressed toward homewater to spawn. Weirs and dragnets snared them. Off Tatoosh Island, Indians trolled for salmon and set hooks attached to kelp lines for halibut and cod. They dipped smelt from surf and estuaries in nets, and standing in canoes they swept crude rakes through the water, impaling herring. Bottom fish were caught at Grays Harbor "by means of the feet," to quote an early-day Indian agent. The Indians simply waded until they stepped on a fish, then picked it up and tossed it into a basket, "the whole procedure enlivened by much splashing and laughing."

The poor and decrepit Indians ate barnacles. The Clallam women gathered limpets ready-cooked by covering them with seaweed and hot rocks. Clams required only a digging stick and an untiring back, and one kind or another abounded on practically every beach.

Potlatching: More than anything else, potlatching distinguished Northwest Indian culture. A potlatch solemnized the significant—the coming of age of a young person, a marriage, a birth, a death. On its lavishness rested the prestige of the host and the entire village.

Guests at Olympic Peninsula potlatches came from as far as the Oregon coast and Vancouver Island, fantastic distances figured at a paddling rate of two to six miles per hour. A Smithsonian report describes a Twana potlatch in 1876 with twelve hundred guests from twenty-two tribes. Preparations took years, the Indian agent safeguarding boxes of wealth until there were enough to be a credit to the Twanas. They built a special potlatch house three hundred feet long and feted their guests for eight days. Women gave away ten thousand yards of calico and men gave three thousand dollars in cash, plus uncounted blankets and canoes. They impoverished themselves, but the largesse of the land assured eventual replacement. So did the potlatch system; the host at one potlatch was guest at the next!

Indians Today: Tradition still lingers on the west coast reservations of the Peninsula. Tribal elders prefer to speak their own tongue, although most of them know English. At LaPush and Taholah a few men still hollow cedar logs into canoes, roughing out the shape with a chain saw and squaring the stern to hold an outboard motor. Women twine baskets of cedar bark and bear grass to give to each other and to sell to tourists. Occasionally, especially at Neah Bay, dancers whirl and lunge to the throb of deer hide drums, and singers lift their voices in the old quavering rhythms.

QUILEUTE INDIAN FISHING

COAST AT LAPUSH

DISCOVERY

The first seamen along the Olympic Coast on a deliberate voyage of discovery may have been Buddhist monks from China, although their voyage is one of those too conjectural to accept, yet too substantiated to dismiss. Chinese court records for the year A.D. 499 tell of a missionary trip led by a monk named Hwui Shan. He followed around the Pacific rim northward from China past Kamchatka, across to the Aleutians, and southward ultimately to Mexico. His report includes accurate geographical details and comments on the customs of peoples visited at the beginning and end of the trip. Unfortunately there is no mention of the two thousand miles between the Aleutian Islands and Baja California. Landfalls must have been made, possibly along this coast; but no one can know where. China had four-decked junks at that time, powered by twelve sails of plaited bamboo and manned by crews of six hundred men. Such vessels regularly plied trade routes south of China and were capable of crossing the Pacific.

Spanish and English: The generally acknowledged discoverer of the Olympic Peninsula is Juan de Fuca, who came eleven centuries after Hwui Shan may have. His case is equally questionable.

For centuries the navigators of Europe sought the fabled Northwest Passage to simplify trading with the Orient. De Fuca, a Greek who sailed under the Spanish flag, boasted of finding it in 1592. His claim is disputed, but the strait north of the Olympic Peninsula lies essentially at the latitude he gave.

Whether de Fuca spoke truly or lied, the Spanish flag first flew here. In August, 1774, Juan Perez sailed up the coast and sighted Mount Olympus. He named it *Santa Rosalia,* the first Caucasian place name in the later state of Washington. The following summer Bruno Heceta dropped anchor south of Point Grenville and rowed ashore with three men to raise the cross of possession for King Carlos III.

These Spanish expeditions were not unnoticed by the British who for two hundred years had claimed the North American coast by virtue of Sir Francis Drake's voyage. In 1776 Captain James Cook was ordered to explore as far as latitude 65° North, and to locate the illusory strait from the Pacific to Hudson's Bay. Benjamin Franklin pleaded safe passage for him, pointing out that Cook's purpose did not conflict with the American colonies' budding revolution.

Cook sailed from Plymouth on July 12, 1776. Two years later he arrived off the Oregon coast and set course northward. On March 22, 1778, he passed Cape Flattery without seeing the entrance to the Strait. His log for that date reads: "This very latitude where we now are is where geographers have placed the pretended Strait of Juan de Fuca; but we saw nothing like it."

The Fur Trade: Expeditions crowded each other in the 1780's, partly because of national interests and partly because of the fortunes to be made in the sea otter trade. Accounts tell of five thousand sea otter skins taken on a single voyage and sold in Canton, China, for $160,000. Another voyage is said to have made a profit three times that great.

James Hanna and James Strange, Englishmen who came in 1785 and 1786, were probably the first fur traders. In 1787, Charles Barclay brought his seventeen-year-old bride, the first white woman to see the Olympic coast.

Next arrived an American, Robert Gray, the mariner on whose discoveries ultimately rested much of the United States claim to the Northwest Coast. In 1788 Gray crossed the mouth of the Strait from Vancouver Island and was met offshore from Neah Bay by Indians in canoes. They had no sea otter skins to trade, but they offered blankets made from the wool of dogs bred specifically for their fleeces. The dogs were the size of terriers, and their wool was compact and long enough to hang from their bellies to the ground. The blankets were coarse and plain, of trade value only as curiosities.

In 1788 two English traders, Charles Duncan and John Meares, sailed up the coast. Duncan drew a map of the Strait, the earliest known. Meares entered the Strait, recognized it as the opening from the sea claimed by Juan de Fuca, and named it in his log "after the original discover."

Both the English and the Spanish centered their Northwest operations at Nootka, midway up the west coast of Vancouver Island. Both built forts there; both conducted a lively trade out from there. In 1789 Spain dispatched an expedition under Estevan Martinez to resolve the conflicting claims of the two nations. The following year a larger expedition sailed under Francisco Eliza charged with the same responsibility. One of Eliza's lieutenants, Manuel Quimper, landed at Neah Bay and explored the Strait. Two years later Eliza's other lieutenant, Salvador Fidalgo, returned and established a fort at Neah Bay, the first European settlement on Washington shores.

That same year, 1792, Captain George Vancouver also arrived, and with him an end to the territorial dispute. Vancouver entered the Strait, meticulously charting. He found Puget Sound and explored it, then turned north and sailed around Vancouver Island to Nootka. He landed with comprehensive knowledge of the Northwest Coast and proceeded to negotiate resolutely with Juan de la Bodega y Quadra, insisting that a treaty already signed between Spain and England should now be carried out in full.

It was the end for the Spanish on this coast. By 1795 they had withdrawn and the British Union Jack flew alone for twenty-three years until it was joined by the American Stars and Stripes. In 1846 a treaty between England and the United States finally ended the century of conflict, and the American flag flew alone.

NORTH WILDERNESS COAST

TIDEWATER LOGGING

SETTLEMENT

There were no white settlers on the Olympic Peninsula to heed the United States-Canada agreement when it was signed. As late as 1848, two years after the boundary treaty, spars for the British Navy were cut at Discovery Bay instead of on the Canadian side of the Strait, and the Peninsula's first settler simply paddled across from Vancouver Island in 1849 and started fur trapping west of Port Angeles.

Timber: During the next two decades settlement got underway. Port Townsend was platted in 1852, the first townsite on the Peninsula, strategically situated at the doorway to Northwest development. Within a few years ships sailed into Puget Sound in such numbers that Port Townsend became an official port of entry and Great Britain, France, Germany, Norway, Sweden, Chile, and Hawaii opened consulates and agencies.

Timber was the moving force behind the development. It reached symbolically even to the inaugural banquet of Washington's first governor in 1853. The cook called guests to the tables by beating mightily on a logging camp "dinner gong," a rusty crosscut saw hanging from a pole! At the time of the inaugural, rude water-powered mills were turning Peninsula trees into timber at Port Townsend, Port Ludlow, and near Shelton; and that same year the Eastern lumber company of Pope and Talbot started a mill at Port Gamble.

Along Hood Canal six-yoke teams of oxen with a pair of bulls as wheelers snaked logs out of the forest. They could drag forty or fifty thousand board feet per day the short distance from falling ground to tidewater. Oddly enough a major threat to their efficiency was yellow jackets. One sting wrecked the discipline of a whole team as frenzy spread from the stung ox to the rest.

Logging crews hailed largely from Maine or Michigan, experienced woodsmen lured West by timber two hundred feet tall and fifteen feet in diameter. They were specialists.

"Fallers" worked from springboards, planks hooked into notches as high as twenty feet up the trunk of a tree. They were unsteady platforms but eliminated three or four feet of hard sawing by enabling the logger to get above the swollen base and main pitch seams of a tree. Even with springboards, fallers sometimes had to cut a great wedge from a tree and creep within its hollow before their fourteen-foot saws could reach through the trunk. The chips from such giants filled a wagon, and the high stumps were monuments both to nature's grand scale and to man's determination. A picture taken along the Satsop River in early logging days shows twenty-eight people standing on top of a Douglas-fir stump!

"Buckers" cut fallen trees into the standard twenty-four-foot lengths most readily handled by the bullteams. Slopes directly above tidewater were fantastically dangerous and teams were not used. Instead a tree was jacked and turned and trimmed until it was free enough to hurtle into Hood Canal. Branches, themselves the size of trees considered fit timber where the men came from, sometimes fell on a bucker and crushed him. Or a log catapulted downhill instead of sliding, or rammed standing trees and sent them toppling like a row of dominoes set on end.

Skid roads eased the process of hauling logs from woods to booming grounds away from the water. "Adzemen" cut crosspieces of hemlock and spaced them eight feet apart, mortising them with maple. To further the dragging of logs, "skid greasers" walked close behind the bullteams, ahead of the loads, daubing the slideways with grease.

By the 1880's sounds of enterprise ended forever the wilderness silence of the lowlands of the Peninsula. Mills had proliferated on the Hood Canal side, and saws were beginning to scream their way into logs at Port Angeles, Port Crescent, and Grays Harbor. Steam power had arrived in the woods.

The donkey engine developed in the redwood country moved north in 1882, and with it came steam railway locomotives. It was the end of the bullteams. The "donkey," which was stationary, yarded logs from where they were cut and bucked; the "lokey" pulled them on flatcars to booming ground or mill.

Ships powered by steam plied scheduled runs between Seattle and Olympia and lumber ports along Hood Canal and the Strait, and soon railroad talk began. Union City felt so assured of a link with Tacoma that in 1892 land along the great bend of Hood Canal sold for one thousand dollars an acre. Port Townsend men laid steel heading for Portland, Oregon. The tracks reached Quilcene, twenty-five miles south of Port Townsend, just in time for the financial panic of 1893. There they ended as backers withdrew their money. Port Angeles was confident that the railroad would come across the north end of the Peninsula and to secure right of way two half-lengths of rail were spiked to crossties on a hillside above Lake Crescent.

When the railroad finally became reality it was at the base of the Peninsula, to Aberdeen. Later it also arrived by railroad ferry across the Sound to Port Townsend, and on to Port Angeles.

Exploring the Mountains: Until 1890 maps of the Olympic Peninsula were blank in the middle. The coastlines had been charted for a century and settlement had dotted the lowland forest for forty years; but no one

knew what lay within the outer rim of the mountains visible from the sea.

Men from Fort Townsend started building a trail across the Peninsula in 1882, but after five months, still in the foothills, they quit. Lieutenant Joseph O'Neil led an exploration into the interior in 1885, but about the time he topped the first range, a courier brought orders temporarily transferring him to Fort Leavenworth, Kansas. The men named their stopping point "No Place," and abandoned the project.

In 1890 a party of five civilian adventurers financed by the Seattle *Press* finally breached the ramparts. James Christie, an ebullient and only slightly experienced young man, led the expedition. Winter was the time to start, he decided, and the route was up the Elwha River by boat. When spring melted the snow and returned the land to green, the *Press* Party would be in the mountains ready to explore the high country.

Diaries reveal the impracticability of the plan. "January 14," reads one. "We have made today not more than a quarter mile, but every foot was worked for and honestly won." The words were penned on a day when the party had made three portages, fought two rapids, and chopped through a submerged log. The temperature was 16° F. and the splashing of the river sheathed both men and boat with ice.

Late in January the men abandoned the boat and contrived sledges to pack their fifteen hundred pounds of supplies. None held together for more than half a mile, but the men were undaunted. "If we can't reach a certain place of vantage today we'll come as near as we can to it, and then get there tomorrow," Christie wrote.

On April 24, five months after leaving Seattle, the explorers climbed a divide at the head of the Elwha Valley and saw below the Quinault Valley, the route to the Pacific. Four weeks later, May 20, 1890, they stepped from the forest to the beach at Taholah. They hired a team and soon were "bowling down the beach" to Aberdeen, to the world which was waiting for the *Press* to publish the news of what lay beyond the rim of the Olympics.

The same year the *Press* Party crossed the Olympics Lt. O'Neil again led an official exploration. This time he went by steamer to Lilliwaup, on Hood Canal, and from there up the Skokomish and over to the Quinault; then back. On the way the men climbed Mount Olympus and traced the courses of the major rivers flowing east and south. They reported, "The interior of the Olympics is useless for all practical purposes. It would, however, serve admirably for a national park."

Homesteading: The 1890's and early 1900's brought homesteaders to the Peninsula. The availability of the land was announced throughout the nation and in Europe; Scandinavian immigrants were particularly attracted, many of them settling in the Lake Ozette region. It was lonely among the tall trees, and hard work was the only sure companion—brush to slash, stumps to burn, elk to rout from the orchard. One of the settlers pinpoints his earliest memories as "when I was just big enough to bend up the bow of the ox yoke and slip in the key." Another speaks of "when I was still too young to pole a canoe."

The first routes to the western Olympic Peninsula were either by steamer from Seattle to Clallam Bay and then overland by trail; or via steamer to Neah Bay and then around Cape Flattery and on south by Indian dugout canoe. Many are the tales of homesteaders tying up to an offshore kelp bed to wait out an adverse surf before risking a landing; and of freighting such unwieldy items as a piano or a loveseat up the foaming rapids of the rain forest rivers. Best known of such stories (and true) is that of the kitchen range and John Huelsdonk, the half-legendary "Iron Man of the Hoh." A man of extraordinary strength, Huelsdonk toted an iron stove on his back from the supply center of Forks to his homestead on the upper Hoh River, a distance of twenty-four miles.

RAIN FOREST HOMESTEAD

"He had to," explains one of his sons-in-law. "The river was too high to go by canoe, and there had been a blowdown so getting a horse through all those jackstrawed trees would have meant a lot of work packing and unpacking. So John carried it. But that part about a hundred pounds of flour in the oven shifting and throwing him off balance crossing Dismal Creek—that's pure exaggeration."

Next to unending work, ingenuity made life in the wilderness possible. Homesteaders chinked their chimneys with clay from the riverbanks, then maintained perpetual fires to keep the damp climate from undoing their masonry. To ward off winter's chill they glued layer on layer of newspaper between the hand-adzed planks of their walls and the flowered wallpaper picked from the Sears, Roebuck catalog. They carved wooden shoes, and sawed spruce log rounds to serve as tables and chairs. Since wheels were useless in the roadless underbrush, they fashioned sledges with runners adzed from vine maple; and to save clearing logs that fell across the trail they simply packed earth on each side and drove up and over.

The men sometimes had to "go outside" and take work in a sawmill or salmon cannery to get cash for what they could neither grow nor devise. But mostly the settlers struggled to make their homesteads self-sustaining. They drove turkeys for miles over forest trails to market. They herded cattle down the beaches and swam them around headlands to the river-mouth trading posts where steam freighters called. Sometimes luck brought a cash windfall. One homesteader tells of driving cattle from the Hoh Valley to Port Townsend—a soul-trying, two-week trip through the forest—then of shooting four cougars the afternoon he got home and netting more cash from the bounty and hides than from the sale of his cattle.

The pattern was much the same throughout the Peninsula. Along Hood Canal and parts of the Strait, tidewater logging had provided the initial thrust. But up the eastside valleys of the Duckabush and Dosewallips and Hamma Hamma, on the "prairies" of Dungeness and Ozette and Forks, and up the rain forest valleys of the west coast, it was the hope of farming that drew the settlers.

Economically it was—and is—risky at every step, from clearing the land to marketing its yield. Yet the harshness of "stump farming" seems not to override the beauty of living in the forest between the Olympic Mountains and the sea. Settlers passed on a love of the land so deep that throughout the Peninsula homesteaders' children, and *their* children and grandchildren, are still living where the virgin forest first gave way to white man.

And, remarkably, the whole pioneer saga is a matter of only decades from beginning to end.

Part 2
NATURAL
HISTORY

GEOLOGY

The immensity of geological time is alien to the human mind but change is noticeable in small and scattered ways—a river cutting a new course, a swamp filling in, scree tinkling down a mountain slope. No landscape ever is form*ed,* past tense. All are form*ing* at a slow, steady, unending pace.

The Mountains: The Olympic Mountains are among the youngest in the world. They are craggy, not yet rounded by weathering and erosion. Avalanche runs gouge their sides and streams rush directly to the sea without interfingering tributaries or sweeping meanders. Yet this "young" landscape is one or two million years old, dating from a late Pliocene uplift, and some of the rocks of which it is made are more than one hundred times that old. Rock that originated as sediment on a Cretaceous ocean bottom about one hundred twenty-five million years ago now forms the central peaks, including Mount Olympus (7,965 feet), and magma that flowed from within the earth in Eocene time, fifty million years ago, now makes up basaltic mountains on the north and east of the Peninsula.

The Olympics evidently uplifted as a dome about sixty miles across. The mountains are a welter of peaks and ridges unoriented as ranges, and the valleys radiate in all directions, as spokes from a central hub. Rock sequences in places are upside down from the order in which they originated; or ancient rock tops more recent rock and there is no hint of what happened to the intervening layers. Evidently the present Olympics are the second Olympics, the second time earth forces have shaped these rocks into mountains.

Glaciation: The principal sculptor of the Olympics has been ice. In Pleistocene time a piedmont glacier three thousand feet thick rounded the contours of the low country and shaped the basins of Puget Sound, Hood Canal, the Strait of Juan de Fuca, and Lakes Crescent and Sutherland. Pothole lakes near Bremerton and Shelton formed as it melted, roughly eleven thousand years ago; and erratic granite boulders carried here from Canada during the long centuries of the glacier's advance were strewn on hillsides and in valleys.

Glaciers extended from Mount Olympus for thirty miles or more. The valleys on the west side of the Peninsula are U-shaped in cross section and their side ridges are truncated: classic signs of glaciation. Moraines impound Lake Quinault and Lake Cushman, although a man-made power dam at Cushman raises the level of the lake far above what it was when

19

ICEFALL, UPPER BLUE GLACIER

dammed only by boulders and silt carried down by the glacier.

Throughout the high country, horn peaks and knife ridges are evidences of the quarrying and plucking of glaciers, and rocks are grooved and polished where ice moved against them. Most of the mountain lakes are *tarns,* lakes lying in basins scooped by ice; and the natural amphitheaters at the heads of valleys are *cirques,* basins in which glaciers gathered mass and began to inch downslope.

It is the building up of snow that forms glaciers. A depth of one hundred feet or more will compact into ice and begin to move, splitting into great crevasses and heaving up *seracs* (jagged ice pinnacles) as the ice is forced to accommodate to the irregularities of the mountain-side.

CREVASSES, LOWER BLUE GLACIER

HOH GLACIER, MOUNT OLYMPUS

In the high Olympics the climate is mild even in winter, but the snowfall is prodigious. In one year scientists on the Blue Glacier measured 450 inches of snowfall which settled around them in an icy blanket thirty feet thick—and that was a year of scant precipitation! Annual snowfall sufficiently exceeds the annual rate of melting that glaciers would probably reform in the Olympics if those existing now somehow disappeared.

Fifty or sixty glaciers now whiten the mountains the year around. Seven are on Mount Olympus, with ice as much as nine hundred feet thick. The longest is the Hoh which stretches for three and one-half miles from its cirque high on Olympus to its snout well below timberline. Only the Blue Glacier has been studied in detail. Its forward movement is about five inches per day, averaged over the year, and as is true of all Olympic glaciers it is annually melting back several feet more than it is advancing. The action is rather like that of an ever-shrinking conveyor belt, continuously moving down the mountain but at the same time shortening its reach into the valley each year.

The Seacoast: Nowhere is the changing nature of the land more apparent than at the seashore. The surf quarries headlands with incessant washing and tunneling, and compresses air within cracks so much that rock loosens and falls as if blasted. Waves strike this coast with a fury unchecked across five thousand miles of the open North Pacific. They hit with a force of two tons per square inch.

Land erodes into the sea; it also rises from it. Photographs of Dungeness taken seventy years ago depict a wharf ending at a building that now stands one mile inland. At Grays Harbor, the children of property owners who bought beach lots at the turn of the century must hike before they can dig clams or swim: geologic change marked on a human time scale. Land is accreting, building up as the coastline rises and sand shifts and fills in. Who properly owns the "new" land is a legal problem not yet resolved.

Many of the islets studding the Olympic coast are "resurrecting." Five times this coast has been flooded by the ocean; five times raised and drained. The islands today were islands in the past. They erode from the land with ready-made roundness, because of the action of bygone waves, and with "nips" notching their sides where ancient surf smashed against them.

Such seastacks are the joy of photographers and the bane of hikers who must climb up and over those not yet fully cut from the land. Many are capped with rock and silt worn from the mountains by glaciers and deposited around the "islands" during a period of elevation above the ocean. The glacial nature of this fill shows in cross section in the necks of land still tying some of the seastacks to the shore. This same relatively recent, fertile sediment is set off sharply from the ancient, sterile rock of the islets themselves by the bright green plant growth that crowns the off-shore stacks.

The contest between water and rock, evident everywhere along the Olympic coast, is most vivid in the tunneled walls of the headlands. At Cape Elizabeth there is a fin of banded sandstone with a wave-cut tunnel through which homesteaders once drove their cattle to the railhead at Moclips. At Elephant Rock and at Point of Arches the sea has lapped and pounded offshore rocks into clustering arches, some of stupendous proportions, others mere needle-eye slits. At Cape Flattery nine adjoining sea caves hollow one wall of a tight cove, most of them high enough to shelter two-story buildings.

The caves and tunnels are dank. Fresh water trickles over their faces and in winter freezes into mammoth icicles which fall and shatter with rifle-shot cracks. At flood tide, waves surge against the rock, relentlessly wearing the tunnels larger. At ebb tide, water shimmers in still pools and barnacles hiss and bubble as they close their plates to await the return of the sea. A sense of the primordial pervades; the shaping and reshaping of the earth is continuous.

SEASTACKS, POINT OF ARCHES

PLANTS

About one thousand species of plants grow on the Olympic Peninsula, giving it the look of a green shag rug tossed between the solid rock and ice of the mountains and the endless shimmer of the ocean. There are all shades of green: the emerald of eelgrass in the tidepools, the creme de menthe of vine maple in the rain forest, the black-green of spruce and cedar, the gray-green of lichen.

Rain Forest: Life's inexorable continuity keynotes the rain forest. New life springs from old and cushions every square foot. Ankle-deep woodsorrel and beadruby, waist-high fern and huckleberry, carpet the forest floor. Spruce and hemlock seedlings inch up from moldering logs. Colonnades of trees with trunks now six to eight feet in diameter survive from starts on logs. Some are six hundred years old, yet their stilted buttresses hold the shape of the nurse log over which their roots first pressed toward the earth.

RAIN FOREST MAPLE　　　　　　　　　　　　　　**NURSE LOG**

The term "rain forest" is new here. Strictly speaking it applies only to tropical forests, which are dominated by broadleaf trees and woody vines and have poor, claylike soil. Olympic rain forests, belonging to the temperate zone, are primarily evergreen and so rich in humus that it takes over two feet of digging to penetrate the forest duff. Yet the two forests have much in common. Superabundant rainfall produces them both —at least eighty inches of rainfall, by definition, and usually one hundred to one hundred fifty. Trees grow unusually tall in both forests. Their trunks convey a feeling of Gothic stateliness and their crowns form a canopy beneath which flourish two other distinct layers of growth. Both forests are undisturbed by wind. Dark. Silent. Lush.

The ocean-facing valleys of the Olympic Peninsula are clothed with rain forest—especially the Hoh, Queets, and Quinault (and the Bogachiel and Calawah to a somewhat lesser extent). Year-round mild temperatures are assured these valleys by the warm Japanese Current flowing just offshore, and up to one hundred seventy-five inches of rain may fall in a single year.

The topmost growth layer, nearly three hundred feet above the ground, is chiefly Sitka spruce and western hemlock intermixed with Douglas-fir and western redcedar and a scattering of black cottonwood. The middle layer is mostly red alder and bigleaf maple. Tangles of vine maple, elderberry, and salmonberry are next; and logs matted with liverworts and tree seedlings, and blankets of moss, deer fern, foamflower, bedstraw, bunchberry dogwood, and myriad other species. Even the air is green! Mosses and maple leaves glow as if lit from within. On cloudy days the whole forest has the soft pervasive light of a cathedral. Only the river bars are dominantly gray, and even there plant pioneers such as sedge and rumex tinge the sand with green.

Lichens and mosses grow on tree trunks; ferns perch in crooks of branches; clubmosses hang in three-foot draperies; even twigs are upholstered. About ninety species of plants have been found in the Hoh Rain Forest growing epiphytically in trees. They use their hosts only as toeholds. Rain supplies moisture and washes down nutrients.

The ideal growing conditions of the rain forest have produced trees that rank among the largest in the world: a western redcedar near Kalaloch that is over 21 feet in diameter; a Douglas-fir in the Queets Valley, nearly 15 feet; Sitka spruce with 13½-foot diameters in the Hoh; a western hemlock in the upper Quinault, over 8½ feet; a red alder in the Hoh, nearly 3 feet. Among the conifers heights of 200 or 250 feet are common and some tower 300 feet, equivalent to 25-story buildings!

Mountain Wildflowers: Rigorous conditions force mountain plants to sprout, grow, fruit, and die within weeks. From July to September flowers color the slopes: yellow cinquefoil and glacier lilies, purple lupine, red paintbrush, white valerian, and bistort. Avalanche lilies, the heralds of

AVALANCHE LILIES

alpine spring, may bloom at the edge of late snowbanks while nearby blue gentians signal the end of summer.

Temperatures within growing plant tissue are as much as 27° F. warmer than the surrounding environment, which allows growth to begin before spring arrives. Sunlight penetrates as much as a foot of snow and permits photosynthesis. The first red stalks of springbeauty plants show beneath icy crusts each June, and lilies commonly push through two or three inches of snow to blossom.

On windswept slopes snow blows off almost as soon as it falls, which foreordains an earlier arrival of spring than on slopes where it piles deep. Soil often is shallow and dry on these slopes, and plants endure the full force of sun and wind. Instead of knee-deep gardens, flowers are scattered and low. Mats of phlox and Douglasia are typical, so is Olympic onion, growing widespaced and with only one blossom per plant.

A few species grow only in the Olympic Mountains, nowhere else on earth. Such plants, known to only one locality, are termed *endemics*. Botanists once thought that the high Olympics harbored nineteen endemics but recently some of these were found on other mountains and the list reduced to eight species, including such choice flowers as Piper bellflower, Flett violet, and a daisylike senecio that grows only on Mount Angeles.

These species are preglaciation relicts. They grew above the ice in Pleistocene time and managed somehow to withstand the increasing cold as the glaciers advanced, and the returning warmth when the ice retreated centuries later.

DEER   BEAR CUB   MOUNTAIN GOAT

WILDLIFE

Two groups of mammals are listed for the Olympic Peninsula—the sixty species that are here, and the eleven that should be but are not. Grizzly bears, wolverines, red fox, lynx, mountain sheep, mountain goats, porcupines, golden-mantled ground squirrels, pikas, water voles, and bog lemming mice never have been native in the Olympics even though they are— or were—common in the Cascade Mountains where conditions are essentially the same.

The reason for the "missing eleven" dates from the Pleistocene ice age. A glacier advancing out of Canada cut off the Olympic Peninsula from the rest of Washington, leaving only its peaks rising above the ice. They were suitable as habitats but as isolated as islands in a sea. Animals simply did not cross the frozen waste that stretched between the Cascades and the Olympics; nor have the eleven thousand years since the ice melted been long enough for them to come.

Eventually most species probably will, except for those such as the grizzly bear and wolverine which are close to extinction. Porcupines and fox have spread naturally as far as the southern base of the Peninsula, and fox introduced near Dungeness from a fur farm have adapted to the wild. Mountain goats introduced in the 1920's are thriving in the inner Olympics.

Elk and Deer: By 1909 excessive hunting threatened West Coast elk with extinction. To protect the species Theodore Roosevelt established a national monument as a refuge in the Olympics in 1909. Enlarged, it now is Olympic National Park.

Elk on the Peninsula probably number over five thousand at present, the largest herd of its kind anywhere. High Divide, Cream Lake Basin, and Anderson Pass are the best places to watch for them in the high country; the river valleys of the Elwha, Bogachiel, Hoh, Queets, and Quinault are the best locations in the low country. Bands of ten to one hundred elk may trail across a meadow to a tarn for the last drink of the day; or in fall they may smash through a lowland vine maple thicket, bugling and snorting and snapping twigs. Either way, an old cow picks the route while a bull stomps at the rear, swishing his five-foot antlers and pretending to be boss!

Bulls are five feet high at the shoulder and weigh seven hundred to one thousand pounds. Cows are about three-fourths as large. Both are brown

ELK IN THE RAIN FOREST

with almost black necks and shoulders, and light rump patches that fairly glow in contrast with the somber hues of the forest.

Blacktail are the only species of deer on the Peninsula. Their hoof marks pit the sand of the beach, the forest mud, and the mountain snow, for they range from low to high country according to season, much as elk do. Buck deer stand about three feet at the shoulder and weigh one hundred fifty pounds. Does are slightly smaller. Their tails are black on the upper side, as the name implies, but white underneath which makes a showy flag as they bound through the forest in alarm.

Mountain Goats: Goats are not native in the Olympics. They are among the "missing eleven" species that never crossed from the Cascades. Wildlife officers traded elk calves that had been hand-raised by a homesteader's daughters in the Hoh Valley for twelve mountain goats from Canada and Alaska which they released on the peaks behind Lake Crescent and in the Elwha Valley. Today there are about one hundred twenty goats in the Olympics, found at the points of original release and also on Mount Angeles, Blue Mountain, Mount Constance, Anderson Pass, and near the Flapjack Lakes.

Mountain goats are about the size of domestic goats and look similar, but they actually are one type of antelope, not members of the goat family. Both billies and nannies have horns; both are an off-white color.

Bear: The only species of bear on the Peninsula is the black bear, and they are found only in the black color phase. Elsewhere "black" bears may be brown or cinnamon or honeycolored; but in the Olympics "black" bears are black. No one knows why.

Bears range from the beaches to the peaks, and even venture occasionally onto the glaciers. They usually take fright at the first glimpse of man, but some have chosen the easy living of campground garbage cans and have become bold, the fate of full-time beggars. Food should be kept out of their reach and they never should be approached or teased.

An exceptionally large male may be six feet long and weigh almost five hundred pounds, but usually they are about half this size. Females are almost as big as males.

Cougars and Bobcats: The Olympic Peninsula has the heaviest cougar population density in the United States, but they are extremely shy of man. Hikers often find cougar tracks in the trail, but almost never see the big cats themselves.

A male cougar is the size of a female African lion—six to eight feet long and about two and one half feet high at the shoulder. They weigh eighty to two hundred pounds. Females are about half the size of males. Both sexes have unspotted fur ranging in color from tawny to gray; both have long tails tipped with black.

Bobcats are less than one-fourth the size of cougars. Their fur is brown and spotted, and their tails stubby. They are more common on the Peninsula than cougars. A trapper took sixty-three bobcats within a five-mile radius of Forks during a single spring.

Marmots: Marmots are the woodchucks of the Western mountains. Their shrill whistle of alarm and the sight of them sitting on the packed-earth "porches" of their burrows, are among the hallmarks of the high country.

They may tunnel up through three or four feet of snow to emerge from hibernation as soon as sprouts are available to feed on, and conversely they withdraw from active life in September or early October while days are still sunny and seed heads are available for food.

MOUNTAIN BEAVER	MARMOT	RACCOON

Olympic marmots are larger and lighter in color than those in the Cascades. They measure seven inches at the shoulder and weigh up to eighteen pounds. Their fur is honey-brown and so thick that it ripples as they bound across a flower field. Their tails are as long as their bodies and as furry.

Mountain Beavers: Here is a misnamed animal! Mountain beavers are not beavers and on the Peninsula they live as much in the lowlands as in the mountains. Sometimes they are called "boomers," mistakenly credited with the drumming noise made by a mating grouse; sometimes they are called "whistlers," confused with marmots; and Lewis and Clark called them "sewellels," assuming that the Indian word for blankets made from the fur was also the word for the rodent.

Mountain beavers are found only from the Northwest south to the Sierra. They are an ancient form of mammal, little changed in the last one million years if the evidence of fossils may be believed. Their burrows are common on moist slopes and they feed so voraciously on young tree growth that foresters consider them a major threat to timber production.

They are about a foot long when full-grown and weigh two or three pounds. Their fur is a coarse gray-brown, their eyes are tiny and ineffectual, their ears hairless and round, and their tails a furry stub.

Small Mammals: Raccoons and skunks are frequent night marauders, especially along Pacific beaches. An 1889 report mentions sixty skunks feeding on crabs and marine worms during a single low tide.

Douglas squirrels, or chickarees, bombard lowland trails with spruce and fir cones cut from the tree tops. Cone hordes a foot or more across are sometimes found, usually by a stream where moisture holds them closed and keeps in the seeds. Studies show that smell, not memory, guides the squirrels back to their caches.

Deer mice are everywhere, their adaptation phenomenal. Shrews abound in the forest, nosing through the duff and eating more than their body weight in insects and grubs each day. Beaver and otter are common; muskrats, mink, and marten less so. Commercial fur trappers' reports for the Peninsula show about twenty-five thousand dollars' worth of pelts taken each year.

Marine Mammals: Gray whales spout and roll close enough inshore to be seen from Olympic Peninsula beaches during their annual migration between California and Alaska. Humpback and little piked whales swim about a half-mile offshore. Porpoises, also in the whale family, sometimes are seen in lagoons and in the Strait.

Steller sea lions stop on the offshore islands while migrating. Their bark carries for miles, sounding like an outboard motor struggling against the current. Harbor seals feed on fish and mollusks, and often rear their heads and shoulders above the water to watch people on the beach. Fur seals migrate five to one hundred miles offshore and rarely are seen except by fishermen.

Sea otters once were abundant, particularly from Grays Harbor to Point Grenville, but the last of them on the Olympic coast were killed about 1900. Their pelts brought as much as $2,500 each. Some day they may return to this coast from colonies in the Aleutian Islands or California, but currently they are only a memory.

Birds: From scoters bobbing by the hundreds in ocean swells to rosy finches skimming above the ice of Mount Olympus, birds claim the full range of the Olympic Peninsula. Eighty-two species are year-round residents; almost two hundred twenty more are visitors or migrants.

During nesting season, daylight in the forest is greeted and dismissed by a forte chorus of robins and juncos plus the hammering of red-shafted flickers, the plaintive minor of varied thrushes, and the raucous call of ravens. Throughout the day warblers, vireos, kinglets, chickadees, finches, and other small birds twitter as they feed right side up and upside down in the tree tops, more easily heard than seen. On the forest floor, winter wrens dart about like minute bundles of brown feathers, and sparrows flit and sing in brush piles along the rivers.

The cry of loons occasionally drifts with the mist across lowland lakes such as Ozette, or the call of a great blue heron cuts the silence as it flaps aloft from a marsh on wings as long as its legs. Kingfishers patrol rivers; harlequin ducks shoot the rapids; and ouzels bob and dip in a jerky ballet from rocks, then walk underwater and feed on the river or lake bottom as though they had forgotten to be birds.

HORNED LARK NEST

In the mountains, horned larks nest on the ground sheltered only by sedge tussocks or stones. Olive-sided flycatchers swoop after insects from the tips of alpine firs, then return to swoop again. Nuthatches pick insects from crevices in the bark of trees; sparrow hawks war against grasshoppers; swallows and swifts dart overhead.

Almost half of the bird species on the Olympic Peninsula are waterfowl, seabirds, and shorebirds. Through the winter the salt water is dotted with brants, buffleheads, grebes, golden eyes, mallard, teal, and a host of others. Their cries and the squeak of wings are sounds of the shore as surely as the lap of the waves. Murres and shearwaters migrate offshore by the thousands each spring and fall. Auklets, puffins, and petrels nest on offshore rocks, coming in such numbers that Coast Guardsmen on Destruction Island counted fifty-six birds killed in a single summer night by flying into the lighthouse beacon.

On the beach dunlins, sanderlings, plovers, sandpipers, and turnstones race up and down and feed at the waves' edge, and black oystercatchers stand knee-deep in seaweed prying not oysters, but mussels off rocks to feed upon. Gulls and cormorants stay the year around, fishing at river mouths and riding the current on bits of flotsam.

Bald eagles, rare throughout the country, here hunch on tall snags along the wilderness beach and soar beyond the curl of the waves, watching for fish and screaming their cry of dying freedom.

CORMORANT   **GULL**

GULLS AT SUNSET

Part 3
ROAD GUIDE

MAP 2 JOINS HERE

To Forks

101

15 △
Kalaloch

Queets

OCEAN

Elephant
Rock

109

Cape
Elizabeth

Taholah

△ 4

Pt. Grenville

109

Moclips

Pacific Beach

PACIFIC

Copalis
Beach

109

Ocean City

2 △

Ocean
Shores

109

Clearwater

River

16 ✗

River

13 △   River   14 ✗

Queets

QUEETS

RAIN

FOREST

101

HIGLEY PK. △

O.N.P.

Lake
Quinault

Amanda Park

To Quinault Rain Forest

Raft

River

QUINAIELT

Duck   Creek

INDIAN

Quinault   River

RESERVATION

101

3 △

▽ Humptulips

River

Humptulips

101

▽

▽

109

101

Hoquiam

River

Wishkah

River

109

GRAYS   HARBOR

101

2 △ Hoquiam

Aberdeen

▽

▽ Westport

105

Cosmopolis

Chehalis   River

410

1 ✗

101

△

To Raymond

To Raymond

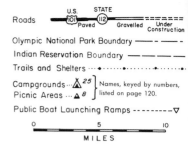

STRIP MAP LOCATION

MAP 1

SCENIC DRIVES

QUEETS RAIN FOREST: River views, fine rain forest, elk, deer; part of Queets Corridor, a strip of Olympic National Park that stretches from glaciers to surf.

QUINAULT RAIN FOREST: Exceptionally pretty forest drive, on both the north and south sides of the lake and river; chance of seeing elk and deer.

COPALIS BEACH TO TAHOLAH: High panoramas of the ocean framed by trees; alternating with easy access to broad beaches.

GRAYS HARBOR: Old road west of Humptulips River, close along shore of bay, leads past fishing boats and old docks.

HOQUIAM AND WISHKAH VALLEYS: River-bottom farms and commercial forests; bucolic charm intermingled with frontier.

WHAT TO DO

CLAM DIGGING (low tide): All beaches, except Quinaielt Indian Reservation which is closed to public clamming.

SMELTING: Beach Four, north of Kalaloch.

SURF FISHING: Most beaches except those on the Quinaielt Reservation; especially popular at Beach Four and near Westport.

SALMON FISHING: Westport and Ocean Shores for charters and rental boats.

SHORT HIKES:

Beaches One through Eight: north and south of Kalaloch.

Tidepool and forest walks led by ranger-naturalists (summer only): Kalaloch.

Queets Forest Loop: from campground at end of Queets road.

Nature Trail: near Quinault Ranger Station, south side of Lake.

Box Canyon of Quinault River: on Enchanted Valley trail, ½ mile from end of southernmost Quinault River road.

MAIN SUPPLY CENTERS

Hoquiam; Aberdeen; Cosmopolis.

MAIN CAMPGROUNDS

BEACH: Kalaloch; Ocean City State Park; Twin Harbors State Park.

FOREST: Olallie, Falls Creek, and Willaby Creek on Lake Quinault; Graves Creek; Promised Land.

SPECIAL EVENTS

RANGER-NATURALIST EVENING CAMPFIRES (summer season): Kalaloch.

LOGGERS PLAY DAY (show of lumberjack skills): Hoquiam, September (most years).

GRAYS HARBOR COUNTY FAIR: Elma (east of Aberdeen), August.

SALMON DERBY: Westport, August.

INDIAN CANOE RACES: Taholah to Lake Quinault, Memorial Day.

INDUSTRIAL TOURS

COSMOPOLIS: Weyerhaeuser pulp mill.

HOQUIAM: Grays Harbor Paper Company.

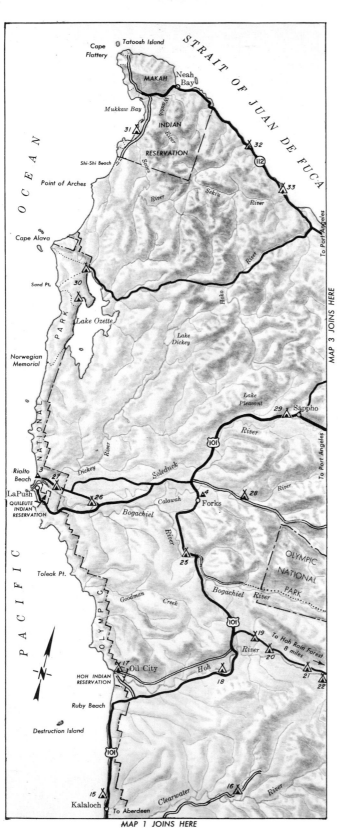

OCEAN

PACIFIC

STRAIT OF JUAN DE FUCA

Cape Flattery
Tatoosh Island
Cape Alava
Sand Pt.
Norwegian Memorial

MAKAH
Neah Bay
INDIAN
RESERVATION
Mukkaw Bay
Shi-Shi Beach
Point of Arches

Waatch River
Sooes River
31
32
33
112

Sekiu River
Hoko River
River

Lake Ozette
PARK
NATIONAL
30

Lake Dickey

Lake Pleasant
29 Sappho
River
101

Rialto Beach
La Push
QUILEUTE INDIAN RESERVATION
3
27
26
Dickey
Soleduck
Calawah
4 Forks
28
River
Bogachiel
23
River

To Port Angeles

MAP 3 JOINS HERE

Toleak Pt.
Goodman Creek
OLYMPIC
NATIONAL
PARK
Bogachiel River

Oil City
17
HOH INDIAN RESERVATION
Ruby Beach
Destruction Island
18
Hoh River
19
20
21
22
To Hoh Rain Forest 8 miles
101

15
Kalaloch
To Aberdeen
Clearwater River
16

MAP 1 JOINS HERE

LEGEND

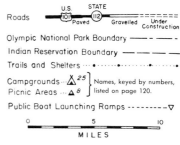

Roads — U.S. 101 Paved — STATE 112 Gravelled — Under Construction

Olympic National Park Boundary — — — -

Indian Reservation Boundary — — —

Trails and Shelters ·•·•·•·

Campgrounds ...△ 25   Names, keyed by numbers,
Picnic Areas ...△ 8   listed on page 120.

Public Boat Launching Ramps - - - - - - ∇

0   5   10
MILES

STRIP MAP LOCATION

MAP 2

SCENIC DRIVES

STRAIT OF JUAN DE FUCA: Overlooks with sweeping views of shipping lane, backdropped by Canada.

LAPUSH: Impressive setting compounded of forest, river, beach, and seastacks; fishing fleet and dugout canoes.

HOH RAIN FOREST: Tall trees, moss draperies, ferns, occasional glimpses of river; watch for elk. 18 miles from US 101 to end of road in Olympic National Park.

WHAT TO DO

SALMON FISHING: Neah Bay; LaPush.

MUSEUM: Hoh Rain Forest, Olympic National Park.

BEACH COMBING: Especially fine on Rialto Beach and Ruby Beach.

SMELTING AND SURF FISHING: Ruby Beach; Beach Four, north of Kalaloch.

CLAM DIGGING (low tide): Kalaloch.

SHORT HIKES:

Tatoosh Island overlook: Cape Flattery (muddy path).

Tidepool walks led by ranger-naturalists at Rialto Beach and Kalaloch; forest walks at Hoh Rain Forest and Kalaloch.

Second and Third Beaches: Accessible by paths from LaPush road.

Nature Trails: Hoh Rain Forest, Olympic National Park.

MAIN SUPPLY CENTERS

Neah Bay; LaPush; Forks.

MAIN CAMPGROUNDS

BEACH: Mora (one mile inland from Rialto Beach); Kalaloch.

FOREST: Tumbling Rapids; Bogachiel State Park; Hoh Rain Forest.

SPECIAL EVENTS

RANGER-NATURALIST EVENING CAMPFIRES (summer season): Mora; Hoh; Kalaloch.

OLD FASHIONED FOURTH (contests, Indian dances, salmon bake): Forks, July 4 (most years).

MAKAH DAY (Indian dances, salmon bake): Neah Bay, late August.

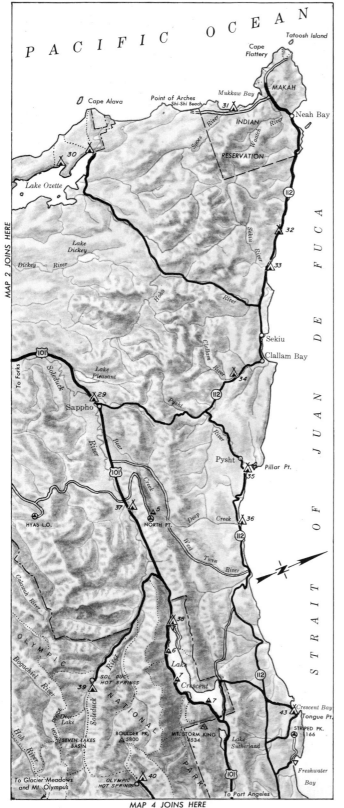

PACIFIC OCEAN

Tatoosh Island

Cape Flattery

Cape Alava

Point of Arches
Shi-Shi Beach

Mukkaw Bay

31

MAKAH

INDIAN

Neah Bay

30

112

RESERVATION

Lake Ozette

MAP 2 JOINS HERE

Dickey   River

Lake Dickey

Ozette   River

Waatch   River

32

Sekiu   River

33

Hoko   River

Sekiu

Clallam Bay

101

To Forks

Soleduck   River

Lake Pleasant

112

34

Pysht   River

29

Sappho

River

101

River

Pysht

Pillar Pt.

Pysht

35

37   5

NORTH PT.

Deep   Creek   36

HYAS L.O.

West   Twin   River   112

Calawah   River

38

6

OLYMPIC

Bogachiel   River

SOL DUC HOT SPRINGS

39

DIVIDE

Lake Crescent

7

Crescent Bay

43   Tongue Pt.

STRIPED PK. 1166

Deer Lake

Soleduck   River

NATIONAL

BOULDER PK. 5800

MT. STORM KING 4534

Lake Sutherland

SEVEN LAKES BASIN

Hoh River

To Glacier Meadows and Mt. Olympus

OLYMPIC HOT SPRINGS   40

PARK

101

Freshwater Bay

To Port Angeles

MAP 4 JOINS HERE

STRAIT   OF   JUAN   DE   FUCA

STRIP MAP LOCATION

MAP 3

SCENIC DRIVES

STRAIT OF JUAN DE FUCA: Road passes through commercial tree farms, climbs overlooks, and sweeps along rocky beaches.

LAKE CRESCENT: US 101 along south shore; spur roads along north shore from each end of Lake.

SOLEDUCK VALLEY: Deep forest and rushing river.

WHAT TO DO

SALMON FISHING: Neah Bay; Sekiu.

MUSEUM (open summer only): Lake Crescent, Olympic National Park.

BEACH COMBING: Agate Beach for agates (privately owned park; small fee).

SWIMMING: Sol Duc Hot Springs (in heated pool).

SHORT HIKES:

Tatoosh Island overlook: Cape Flattery (muddy path).

Soleduck Falls: Forest trail, one mile from end of Soleduck road.

Marymere Falls Nature Trail: Lake Crescent, behind museum.

MAIN SUPPLY CENTERS

Neah Bay; Clallam Bay.

MAIN CAMPGROUNDS

FOREST: Tumbling Rapids; Klayhowya; Fairholm (Lake Crescent); Soleduck.

SPECIAL EVENTS

RANGER-NATURALIST EVENING PROGRAMS (summer season): Fairholm Campfire Circle, Lake Crescent Lodge, and Soleduck Campfire Circle; (all open to the public without charge).

MAKAH DAY (Indian dances, salmon bake): Neah Bay, late August.

MAP 3 JOINS HERE

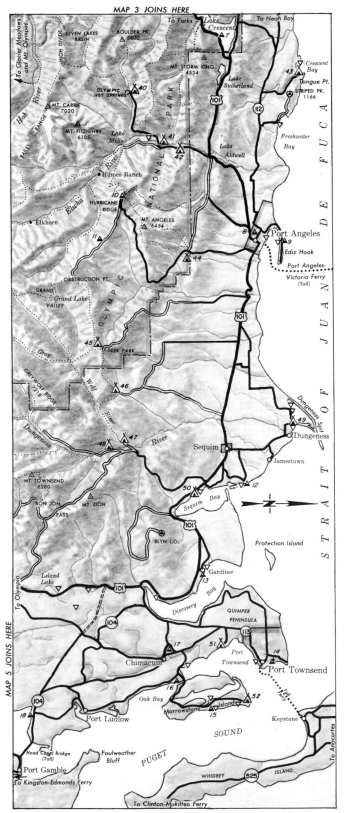

To Glacier Meadows and Mt. Olympus
To Forks
Lake Crescent
To Neah Bay

SEVEN LAKES BASIN
BOULDER PK. 5800
HIGH DIVIDE
7
Crescent Bay
43
Tongue Pt.
MT. STORM KING 4534
Lake Sutherland
STRIPED PK. 1166
Hoh River
MT. CARRIE 7020
OLYMPIC HOT SPRINGS
40
Lake Mills
41
Lake Aldwell
101
112
Freshwater Bay
MT. FITZHENRY 6105
42
Lake Aldwell
Humes Ranch
BAILEY RANGE
NATIONAL PARK
Elwha
10 HURRICANE RIDGE
Elkhorn
MT. ANGELES 6454
11
8
Port Angeles
9
Ediz Hook
Port Angeles-Victoria Ferry (Toll)
44
OBSTRUCTION PT.
GRAND VALLEY
Grand Lake
OLYMPIC
Gray
101
45 DEER PARK
GREYWOLF RIDGE 7218
Wolf River
46
Dungeness
Dungeness Spit
49
47
48
River
Sequim
Jamestown
MT. TOWNSEND 6280
50
12
BON JON PASS
MT. ZION
Sequim Bay
101
BLYN L.O.
Protection Island
STRAIT OF JUAN DE FUCA
Leland Lake
Gardiner
13
101
Discovery Bay
104
QUIMPER PENINSULA
113
MAP 5 JOINS HERE
17
51
14
Chimacum
Port Townsend
104
16
Oak Bay
Port Townsend
18
Port Ludlow
Marrowstone Island
52
15
Keystone
SOUND
Hood Canal Bridge (Toll)
Foulweather Bluff
Port Gamble
PUGET
WHIDBEY ISLAND
525
To Kingston-Edmonds Ferry
To Clinton-Mukilteo Ferry
To Anacortes
To Olympia

STRIP MAP LOCATION

MAP 4

SCENIC DRIVES
LAKE CRESCENT: Both the north and south shores.
ELWHA VALLEY: The road follows close along the river, then climbs to Lake Mills and Olympic Hot Springs.
EDIZ HOOK: Sand spit protecting Port Angeles harbor; beach, views of shipping and log booms.
HURRICANE RIDGE: Alpine meadows; views of peaks and glaciers.
DUNGENESS: Farmland with both marine and mountain views.
MARROWSTONE ISLAND: South of Port Townsend, views across salt water to Olympics and to Cascades.

WHAT TO DO
SALMON FISHING: Port Angeles; Port Townsend.
MUSEUMS: Lake Crescent (open summer only); main Olympic National Park museum in Port Angeles (open all year); County historical museum and Rothschild House, Port Townsend.
CRABBING (low tide): Dungeness, Pillar Point.
CLAM DIGGING (low tide): Sequim Bay State Park; Oak Bay, south of Hadlock.
SKIING, SNOWSHOEING, SLEDDING: Hurricane Ridge, December to March (weekends and holidays only).
SHORT HIKES:
Elwha River Trail: From Altaire Campground to road on the west side of river.
Lake Angeles: Beautiful lake in glacial cirque, above Heart O' the Hills.
Big Meadow: Wildflowers, marmots, and views along Hurricane Ridge.
Hurricane Hill Nature Trail: Commanding viewpoint, wildflowers.
Wildflower walks led by ranger-naturalists daily in summer at Hurricane Ridge; also hikes to Hurricane Hill.

MAIN SUPPLY CENTERS
Port Angeles; Sequim; Port Townsend.

MAIN CAMPGROUNDS
BEACH: Sequim Bay State Park; Fort Flagler State Park.
FOREST: Elwha; Altaire; Olympic Hot Springs; Heart O' the Hills.

SPECIAL EVENTS
RANGER-NATURALIST TALKS (summer season): During the day at the National Park museum in Port Angeles and at Hurricane Ridge; evening campfires at Elwha and Heart O' the Hills campgrounds.
SKIN-DIVING MEET AND OCTOPUS GRAB: Port Angeles, March.
RHODODENDRON FESTIVAL: Port Townsend, April or May.
IRRIGATION DAYS (loggers' rodeo): Sequim, May.
SUMMER SCHOOL OF THE ARTS (University of Washington Extension courses): Port Townsend, June and July.
SUMMER THEATER: Port Townsend.
COUNTY FAIRS: Port Angeles and Port Townsend, August.
SALMON DERBIES: Port Angeles and Port Townsend, August and September.

INDUSTRIAL TOURS
PORT ANGELES: Crown Zellerbach (newsprint); Peninsula Plywood; Rayonier (cellulose).
PORT TOWNSEND: Crown Zellerbach (kraft and paper bags).

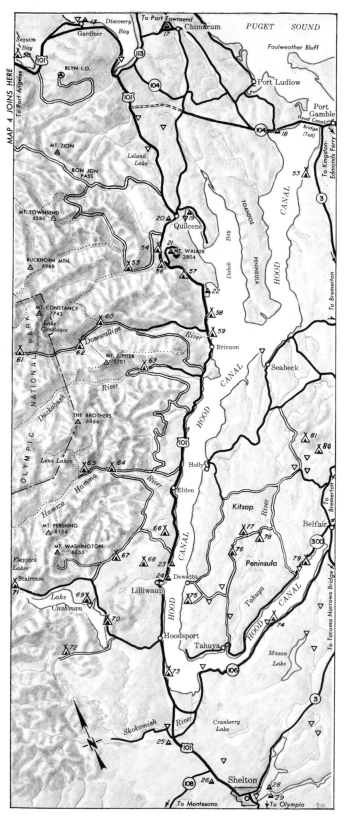

SCENIC DRIVES
HOOD CANAL: US 101 hugs the shores from Brinnon to Belfair.

MOUNT WALKER: Panorama of Olympic Mountains and Puget Sound (gravel road).

DOSEWALLIPS: Forested valley studded with farms.

LAKE CUSHMAN: Forest drive with views of Lake.

OAKLAND BAY: Tidewater log booms, north of Shelton.

WHAT TO DO
CLAM DIGGING: Nearly all public beaches (see Directory for list).

OYSTER PICKING: Many public beaches (see Directory for list).

SALMON FISHING: Shelton; Bremerton; Olympia.

MUSEUM: Naval Museum, Bremerton; State Historical Museum, Olympia.

SHORT HIKES:

Dose Forks: Forest and river trail, from end of Dosewallips road.

Staircase Rapids: Along river beyond ranger station; enormous cedar tree.

MAIN SUPPLY CENTERS
Quilcene; Hoodsport; Shelton. (Bremerton and Olympia, beyond borders of this strip map.)

MAIN CAMPGROUNDS
BEACH: Sequim Bay State Park; Dosewallips State Park; Potlatch State Park; Twanoh State Park; Belfair State Park.

FOREST: Dosewallips (end of the road in Olympic National Park); Lena Creek; Staircase.

SPECIAL EVENTS
MOUNTAINEER PLAYERS (outdoor drama): Shelton, June.

CAPITAL LAKEFAIR (water show): Olympia, July.

KITSAP STAMPEDE (rodeo): Silverdale, near Bremerton, August.

KITSAP AND THURSTON COUNTY FAIRS: Silverdale and Olympia, August.

INDUSTRIAL TOURS
BREMERTON: Shipyards.

OLYMPIA: Georgia Pacific Corrugated Container Co.; Merchant Marine Reserve Fleet; Olympia Brewing Co.; Olympia Cheese Co.

SHELTON: Simpson Timber Co. mills.

NEAR CAPE FLATTERY

ROAD GUIDE

Roads give access to the lowland periphery of the Peninsula, and climb the heights of the outer mountains. The points of interest listed here are on main roads unless noted to the contrary. Remember that the distance between towns calls for planning ahead on gasoline and other travel needs, and that many of the towns shown on maps are scarcely more than cross-road communities.

ABERDEEN: In the 1890's civic leaders called on every man in Aberdeen to work ten days leveling a railroad grade and laying ties, or to donate the equivalent in cash at the rate of two dollars a day. Rails were salvaged by "volunteers" from the hold of a ship that had sunk off Oyehut six years earlier. Old-timers say that they were too pitted from the years on the bottom ever to give a smooth ride, but they sufficed. Tying into the mainline launched Aberdeen and adjoining Hoquiam as the twin city industrial center of Grays Harbor. Today trains and tugboats bring logs out of the forest, and freighters tie up at the mill docks to load lumber.

The name Aberdeen is Scottish for "the meeting of two rivers," in this case the Wishkah and Chehalis. Accommodations, services, and supplies are available in Aberdeen-Hoquiam.

BREMERTON: Shipyards here have repaired Navy vessels since the Spanish-American War; drydock facilities are the largest on the West Coast. To see them, take the hour-long bus tour which departs from the main gate of Puget Sound Naval Station. It operates throughout the year. Highlights are the Naval Museum and the mothballed battleship *U.S.S. Missouri* where the United States accepted the Japanese surrender, ending World War II.

Bremerton is on the Kitsap Peninsula, a projection off the east side of the Olympic Peninsula. Accommodations, services, and supplies are readily available. A scenic drive leads around Sinclair Inlet south of Bremerton; others, along Hood Canal, are not far distant.

CAPE FLATTERY: The very northwest tip of conterminous United States is a high rock promontory battered by surf and scalloped by coves. The road to the Cape begins on the outskirts of Neah Bay and ends at a path leading the last half-mile through the trees and salal to a view of Tatoosh Island. Spur roads lead to radar installations, logging operations, a steep scramble down to the beach, and musty World War II bunkers. The main road is muddy and narrow beyond Makah Air Force station but usually readily passable; the spurs branch confusingly and are likely to be muddy.

CLALLAM BAY: Captain Henry Kellett named this bay in the Strait in 1847, inking it onto his chart as a phonetic rendition of the Makah Indian name for their neighboring tribe, *Klolub Ant,* Clam Men. Clallam Bay was a major port from the 1880's to the 1930's, when a road at last was built along the Strait. Until then settlers on the western Peninsula had no link with the outside world except the trail overland to Clallam Bay and then the steamer to Port Angeles, Seattle, Victoria, or wherever their business called them. Today the village is a supply center for loggers and sport fishermen, and the site of a Coast Guard station. Gasoline, groceries, and accommodations are available.

COPALIS BEACH: The resort communities along the beaches west of Aberdeen-Hoquiam are geared to vacationers' needs. Copalis offers cabins, cafes, shops, even specialty houses with "clam guns" for rent, both the standard, short-handled shovels and the new tubes. Success in digging razor clams here is guaranteed when the tide is low. The beach is smooth and firm enough to drive on.

RAZOR CLAM DIGGING

CRESCENT BAY: In the 1880's and 1890's a town thrived on the flat between the present county park at Tongue Point and the private park at Crescent and Agate beaches. Remnants of the old skid road that led from the falling ground east of the Lyre River to the booming ground in Crescent Bay may be seen in the forest. But early logging towns seldom survived the cutting of the trees immediately at hand, and Port Crescent was no exception. Once it rivaled Port Angeles as the main city on the north Peninsula. Today only its graveyard and its beach remain.

DEER PARK: Here is alpine country with a view north across the Strait to the San Juan Islands and Canada and back toward the ice-crested Olympics. Endemic plants found nowhere else in the world grow in the meadows. Marmots nibble flowers and whistle from their burrow mounds on the slope above the campground. Deer are common. Watch for mountain goats and snowshoe rabbits.

The road turns off US 101 east of Port Angeles. It is unpaved most of the way; narrow, steep, winding—and readily passable for anyone used to mountain driving. Snow usually closes it from October to June.

DESTRUCTION ISLAND: In 1775 Indians killed men from a Spanish ship anchored in the lee of this island as they were getting water from the Hoh River. *La Isla de Dolores,* Island of Sorrows, their commander, Bodega y Quadra, wrote in his log—and popular belief became that the name was commemorative. Actually it was penned the day before the tragedy. The present name came to the island via the river. Twelve years after Bodega y Quadra's men were slain the English explorer Charles Barclay also sent men ashore for water and they too were killed. He gave the river the name "Destruction," and later this was transferred to the island and the river kept its Indian name, "Hoh."

The Destruction Island lighthouse was built in 1885 at the fantastically high cost of $90,000; prices spiraled because of the difficulty of landing materials across the reef and hoisting them up the cliff. Electricity powers the light now, but for years the lighthouse keeper had the nightly chore of carrying ten gallons of kerosene up the ninety-four-foot tower to the beacon.

DISCOVERY BAY: Vancouver and his men rowed to the beach of this bay on March 6, 1792, and, to quote Vancouver's journal, "indulged in a holiday for the purpose of taking some recreation and exercise on shore." It was their first time on land since rounding the Cape of Good Hope! Two years earlier Spaniards under Lt. Manuel Quimper had stopped to refit their ships here and named the bay for Bodega y Quadra, the officer destined to negotiate with Vancouver regarding sovereignty in these waters. But unaware of this, Vancouver named the bay *Discovery,* for his ship.

US 101 and State 113 offer views of the bay; side roads to Gardiner and Diamond Point give access to the water.

DOSEWALLIPS: The road turns off US 101 south of Quilcene at Brinnon and passes a few houses and farms before plunging into the forest. Notice Dose Cascades, a perpetual froth of white near the end of the road, and the adjacent "pillow lava" that issued from fissures in an ancient seabottom and cooled underwater. A pleasant forest trail leads up the Dosewallips Valley beyond the road.

DUNGENESS: According to Clallam Indian tradition the sandspits at Dungeness and Port Angeles were one until the mythical hero, *Kakyhuck,* tired of having to portage across or paddle around it every night on the way home, cut them apart. Half of the great spit drifted east to become Dungeness Hook; half—now known as Ediz Hook—stayed at Port Angeles. Vancouver named Dungeness because the sandspit and tideflats reminded him of Dungeness, England. The word comes from the Anglo Saxon *dene* —sandy—and *naess*—cape.

Early manifest books show that the Dungeness wharf built across the tideflats into the harbor handled a steady flow of goods from the 1880's until after the turn of the century. Butter, eggs, potatoes, rhubarb, baled hay, and cows were shipped regularly to Port Townsend and Port Crescent. Pilings of the old wharf still march into the bay, and a few buildings from Dungeness' days as a port city still stand. But the trade center has shifted to Sequim, on US 101, and Dungeness now is known for its farmlands with views of both the Olympics and the Strait. Roads checkerboard the area, few of them signed but all of them scenic.

DOSE CASCADES/DUNGENESS: COMMERCIAL CRABBING AND OCTOPUS FISHING

ELEPHANT ROCK: The wave-cut rock at the mouth of the Raft River will be accessible by walking and wading when the coast road along the Quinaielt Indian Reservation is completed. The sight and sound of the water surging in its immense arches and caves is one of the delights of the Olympic seashore. Stroll south to the Hogsbacks for pleasant beach scenery —sand, seastacks, and shorebirds.

ELWHA VALLEY: The Elwha River is forty miles long from headwaters near Mount Olympus to outlet in the Strait. Mountain goats graze on the cliffs across the river from the road inside the National Park boundary, and elk feed along the river bottom. A power dam impounds Lake Mills, five miles up the road from US 101. Trails to Humes Ranch, Elkhorn, and Low Divide leave from Whiskey Bend, nine miles from US 101. Beginning in late August spawning salmon enter the Lower Elwha, a part of the river accessible from State 112.

FISH HATCHERIES: Four salmon hatcheries operate on the Olympic Peninsula—at Hoodsport; near Shelton on the Skokomish River; north of Montesano on the Satsop; and south of Sequim on the Dungeness. The best time to visit is between September and December when adult salmon are returning to homewater to spawn. Hatchery men take eggs from the bellies of females and after accumulating about forty thousand in a pan, they strip the milt from two or three males and mix it in by hand. These fertilized eggs are hatched in special trays and the fry are reared to migratory age, then released in streams to start their journeys to the ocean.

In addition to salmon hatcheries there are trout hatcheries on the Peninsula, and salt-water and fresh-water fish farms. All are open to the public although without special provision for guided tours.

FORKS: The first settler in the Forks region was Peter Fisher, a fur trapper and meat hunter who came in the 1860's, lived in a hollow stump,

SALMON FIGHTING UPSTREAM

TROUT FISHING, ELWHA RIVER

and packed out what he garnered by rifle and trapline to sell in Victoria, B.C. The second settler, Luther Ford, arrived ten years later. He had been on the verge of paying four hundred dollars for forty acres of what became the central business district of Seattle, when he decided that fortune lay in Forks land!

Today Forks is the main point of supply and service for the west side of the Peninsula; accommodations, supplies, and limited services are available. The hills behind town are charred and nude because of a 1951 fire. It started on the 109th day without rain, when trees were as combustible as if kiln-dried. In ten hours flames had leaped and crackled across twenty thousand acres. People evacuating the town switched on car headlights although it was noon, so thick was the smoke; and ashes fell like hot snow on the men who stayed behind to hose roofs and try to save their homes. A wind shift diverted the holocaust from the town, but five hundred seventy-five million board feet of timber were lost. Salvaging what was left took three years. The entire sixty square miles have been reseeded but decades are needed to turn the black hillsides to green. To see the devastation drive a few miles on the Calawah-Sitkum road northeast of town.

Ten miles south of Forks is a shingle mill with a log pond right beside the highway and a steam donkey engine still used to unload trucks. Two miles south of it is a field of blue camas, the plant prized by Indians for its starchy bulb.

GRAYS HARBOR: The American mariner Robert Gray discovered this harbor in 1792, after having traded with Indians at LaPush for fish and near Destruction Island for fur. He named it Bullfinch Harbor, for Charles Bullfinch, one of the Bostonian owners of Gray's ship. Subsequently Vancouver named it Gray's Harbor for its discoverer, and this name became accepted because Vancouver's charts were published while Gray's were not.

Aberdeen and Hoquiam bring the smoke and rush of modern industry to the shores of the harbor now, and Westport is a busy commercial and sport fishing village. But for a glimpse backward through history take the side road off State 109 near the mouth of the Humptulips River or drive and walk the muddy ruts south of Ocean Shores to Duck Lake and Damon Point.

HOH RAIN FOREST: The road turns off US 101 south of Forks and winds gently through the forest with views upriver to the mountains. Outside the National Park, fifteen-foot charred stumps still stud pastures, and immense logs lying end to end serve as fences. Inside the Park, museum exhibits explain what "rain forest" is and self-guiding nature trails loop through the forest past nurse logs green with spruce and hemlock seedlings, and beneath canopies of maple boughs hung with clubmoss and lichen and fern. Ranger-naturalists lead walks during the summer season and give evening campfire talks.

To sense the timelessness of this forest, walk alone on one of the trails or out on the river bar. Notice the truly great size of the trees and listen to the silence. Watch for elk and deer.

HOOD CANAL: The name dates from Vancouver's voyage of discovery in 1792. In his journal he wrote: "Early on Sunday morning the 13th of May we again embarked, directing our route down the inlet, which, after the Right Honorable Lord Hood, I called Hood's Channel." But though he wrote "channel" in his journal, Vancouver entered it as "canal" on his chart—and confusion has reigned ever since. Hood Canal is a natural channel, a narrow inlet of Puget Sound reaching thirty-five miles from Port Gamble almost to Shelton and then bending east for another five miles. Samuel Hood, the British admiral for whom Vancouver named the "canal," saw service in the American Colonies; in fact he was rebuked for failing to relieve Cornwallis at Yorktown.

US 101 sweeps close to the water the length of Hood Canal. Public access to the beach makes possible oyster picking and clam digging at several points. The drive is especially beautiful in May and June when rhododendron, dogwood, and madrone are blooming; and in fall when maples and cottonwoods patch the conifer forest with scarlet and gold. In several places the old alignment of US 101 meanders off the new highway like a country lane, winding past cottages and resorts and offering views of

HOOD CANAL

beaches and coves. Hoodsport and Quilcene are the largest settlements.

HOOD CANAL BRIDGE: The State Department of Highways operates a toll bridge across Hood Canal north of Bremerton. It is more than a mile long, the longest salt-water floating bridge in the world. It took three and one-half years to build, cost almost twenty-eight million dollars, and has twenty-three pontoons and forty-two anchors. It opened in 1961.

HOODSPORT: The hatchery here raises young salmon in salt-water ponds and releases them directly into Hood Canal, eliminating the usual migratory stage down a river. The Rayonier Marine Laboratory researches new uses for timber by-products and improvements in pulping processes. Gasoline and groceries are available in Hoodsport; motels and resorts in the vicinity are numerous.

HOQUIAM: Indicative of Hoquiam's role as a timber center is the Log Patrol licensed by the State. Timbermen brand logs much as cattlemen do steers, and they also suffer occasional losses due to rustling. Thieves working the night tides pirate logs from a boom and saw the brand off the end or alter it, a felony subject to a fine of $5,000 or ten years in prison. The work of the Log Patrol is to guard against such rustling and to clear navigation channels of logs gone astray. They salvage two million board feet a year, towing logs to a sorting ground, separating them by brand, and marketing them on a 60/40 basis with the sixty per cent going to the registered owner.

Cranberries grow on some one hundred fifty thousand acres of bogland near Hoquiam, one of three major growing areas in the United States along with Michigan and the coast of Massachusetts. They are processed on a cooperative basis by the Ocean Spray Cranberry Company at Grayland. It is open to visitors during the October and November harvest season.

The Weyerhaeuser Company mill at Cosmopolis, just southeast of Hoquiam-Aberdeen, also is open to visitors. It debarks logs from tree farms on the southern Peninsula, then chips, cooks, and bleaches them for the making of paper.

Hoquiam is an industrial and commercial center with a full range of city services.

HURRICANE RIDGE: No alpine country on the Peninsula is more visited than Hurricane Ridge, a scenic merging of flower meadows, glaciated peaks, and a view across the Strait to Canada. It is a show of color from late June when the first lilies bloom at the retreating edges of snow patches, until October when the huckleberry turns crimson and the azalea turns gold. Deer are common; mountain goats peer occasionally from the cliffs above the road tunnels; marmots scamper along the self-guiding nature trail to Hurricane Hill. A lodge at the summit has a coffee shop and souvenirs but no overnight accommodations. Ranger-naturalists give talks on its terrace in summer, and lead walks through the meadows. The road nine miles east along the ridge to Obstruction Point is highly scenic.

SKIING   **HURRICANE RIDGE LODGE**

WINTER ON HURRICANE RIDGE

In winter snow piles twenty feet deep and winds dispel any doubt about the name "Hurricane" Ridge. The road is plowed open on weekends from December to April; the lodge serves as a warming hut and rents skis, snowshoes, and sleds; rope tows take skiers up the slopes of Big Meadow and to the head of the Little River drainage.

INDIAN RESERVATIONS: Traditional dancing, basketmaking, and fishing from dugout canoes are part of the mainstream of life on the Makah, Quileute, Hoh, Queets, and Quinaielt reservations, on the west coast of the Peninsula, along with church, P.T.A., and TV. Most of the other reservations frequently shown on maps have little that mark them overtly as "Indian"; the Ozette Reservation is abandoned. The Makah and Quileute reservations have tourist accommodations; the others do not. All are privately owned land.

KALALOCH: US 101 hugs the cliff above the beach at Kalaloch (pronounced *Klay'lock*), offering glimpses of ocean through the trees. North

SURF FISHING, BEACH FOUR

and south are beaches designated by numbers from One through Eight, a naming system that breeds confusion with First, Second, and Third Beaches near LaPush. Watch for whales from the height of the bluff, and notice how winds have buffeted the trees into a matted upsweep. The swellings on spruce trees are burls, tumorous cell multiplications of unknown cause, possibly associated with salt air. There are gasoline, groceries, and a lodge at Kalaloch. Ranger-naturalists give campfire programs in summer and lead walks; a museum is to be built. Good razor clamming; smelting and surf fishing at Beach Four.

LAKE CRESCENT: According to Indian legend, Mount Storm King once grew so tired of watching Clallams and Quileutes fight that he broke a rock off his head and rolled it down on them. The rock was so big that it dammed a river and made a new lake. Geologists almost agree with this origin of Lake Crescent! The two-hundred-foot rise that the highway crosses between Lake Crescent and Lake Sutherland is an ancient landslide, composed of rock debris entirely different than the surrounding glacier-deposited material. Evidently when it fell it dammed the Lyre River which at that time flowed east into Lake Sutherland. The rising water of the new lake forced the Lyre to reverse its flow and become an outlet draining into the Strait instead of an inlet draining into the valley.

Lake Crescent is six hundred feet deep. US 101 hugs its south shore for ten miles; branch roads from each end of the lake lead along part of its north shore past cottages and resorts. Watch for families of wild mallard ducks in late spring, and for signs of where beaver have fed on the bark of alder trees. A National Park visitor center and nature trail are midway along the south shore drive. Ranger-naturalist talks are given in summer at Lake Crescent Lodge and Fairholm Campground. Port Angeles is the nearest town.

LAKE CUSHMAN: A dam built in 1926 to supply power for Tacoma backed water from the Skokomish River deep into the mountains, impounding Lake Cushman, a reservoir with a forty-mile shoreline. Mount Washington and Mount Elinor rise spectacularly above it; good fishing for silver trout, sockeye, cutthroat, and bass. Hoodsport is the nearest town.

LAKE OZETTE: In the 1890's a community gained a toehold on the shores of this lake just a mile inland from the ocean. "Those enormous trees . . ." wrote one of the early settlers. "I expect it was foolhardy to try and conquer this forest and change it into farmland. The first thing we did after selecting a place for our own was to fall a big cedar tree for building. It was sixteen feet in diameter near the ground. We set fire to the hollow inside to burn out the dry and rotten parts, then a man could stand inside and one man outside and saw it down."

Some homesteaders built two-story houses with gingerbread eaves and flowered wallpaper. Others built "prove-ups," 12 x 14-foot shanties with crude hatches in the roofs for doors and no windows; mere technical compliances with the homestead law. For a time the community seemed to flourish but isolation took an inevitable economic toll. By the time the road was built in 1924 most of the homesteaders had gone.

Today time rests gently. Lake Ozette remains essentially wild. A few homestead houses still stand; there is a fishing resort; and trails penetrate the dense forest to the beach. The lake is nine miles long, the largest totally natural lake in the state. (Both Lake Chelan and Lake Washington are stabilized by dams.) The west shore of Ozette is in the Olympic National Park.

LAKE QUINAULT: Roads lead along north and south shores of the lake; gasoline and groceries are available in Amanda Park; resorts are on the lakeshore. For a ride down the Quinault River in an Indian dugout canoe, check at Amanda Park or Quinault Lodge. The lake is part of the Quinaielt Indian Reservation and fishing and boating are regulated by the tribal council.

CANOEING, LAKE CRESCENT

CANOE MAKER   **QUILEUTE CHIEF**

LAPUSH: Forest-fringed beaches and wave-lashed islands are the setting of LaPush, a fishing village on the Quileute Indian Reservation. Indians using dugout canoes fish for salmon and smelt in the mouth of the river; trollers tie up at the fish-buying barge to unload catches taken at sea. Gasoline and groceries are available; cafes and resorts cater to sports fishermen and tourists.

The beaches near LaPush are part of Olympic National Park. First Beach is immediately beyond the drift logs and jetty on the oceanward edge of town. Second Beach, with seastacks close inshore and rich tidepools, is reached by a twenty-minute walk through the forest from the highway east of town. Third beach, also reached by trail, has tidepools at its north end, a stream midway down the beach, and a waterfall on the high bluff at its sound end.

The name LaPush is a corruption of *la bouche,* French for "the mouth," referring to the Quillayute River which empties into the Pacific here.

MARROWSTONE ISLAND: Bridges connect Marrowstone Island to the mainland south of Port Townsend. On the island the immediate scene is pastoral, the distant scene spectacular. From Marrowstone's east beaches the Cascade Range rises from the sea with Mount Baker to the north, Mount Rainier to the south. From the west beaches the view is of the Olympics. Tide rips are strong; notice the one-hundred foot wakes streaming behind wharf pilings. Vancouver wrote in his journal that his men could scarcely progress against the current even using both oars and sail.

Fort Flagler, on the north end of the island, now a state park, was built shortly before the Spanish-American War. Its guns were mounted on disappearing carriages which raised above the rampart to fire, then kicked back into the encasement by recoil for reloading.

Gasoline and groceries are available at Nordland.

MOCLIPS: In the early days homesteaders in the Queets Valley drove their cattle down the beach from the mouth of the Queets to Moclips, for railroad shipment to market. Horse-drawn wagons brought clams and fish from Taholah for canning. But today the only industry in Moclips is a sawmill. Clamming is excellent on the beaches; basic tourist needs are met in town. The drive north is scenic.

MOUNT WALKER: Here is a view! Westward stretch the jagged high peaks of the Olympics, snowcapped all year; eastward lie the blue waters of Hood Canal and Puget Sound with Mount Baker, Glacier Peak, and Mount Rainier soaring above the rest of the Cascade Range. Rhododendrons bloom on the summit of Mount Walker in June. The road, which leaves US 101 south of Quilcene, is easy for anyone accustomed to driving off the pavement.

NATIONAL WILDLIFE REFUGES: Sea birds by the thousands nest on the rock islets that dot the ocean coast of the Peninsula, and stop on migration to rest and feed. Ducks and geese winter in the protected waters of Dungeness Hook. To protect them the Fish and Wildlife Service administers refuges which are not open to human intrusion except by special permit.

NEAH BAY: The first white settlement in the state was a fort named Nuñez Gaona built in Neah Bay in 1792 as a provisioning depot for passing Spanish ships. Lt. Salvador Fidalgo commanded the undertaking, expecting to raise vegetables and livestock brought by frigate from Mexico and to build a brick bake oven. But four months after arriving, he was ordered to abandon post. England had forced Spain to relinquish all land north of San Francisco, although Spanish negotiators tried to retain Nuñez Gaona as the northern limit of their domain.

Today Neah Bay is an Indian village and fishing port, as it always has been. Makahs lived by fishing and hunting seals and whales before white men came, and after their arrival trading intensified the Indians' zeal. Eight thousand sealskins per year, valued at two dollars apiece, were shipped from Neah Bay during the 1880's, and thirty thousand gallons of whale oil sold for forty cents per gallon. Whaling and sealing from dugout canoes continued until the 1920's but the taste of whale oil is now only a memory and seals are increasingly rare on Makah tables. None are hunted for the market. Fishing, however, is an economic mainstay. A commercial fleet of trollers and seiners, owned by both whites and Indians, fishes from Neah Bay for salmon and gill netters go after such bottom fish as halibut, sole, and cod. All summer the harbor is lively, but boat owners move to quieter waters in winter, for Neah Bay is exposed to the fury of Pacific storms.

Tourist accommodations are ample the year around; Neah Bay offers the largest supply of Indian baskets and shell jewelry on the Peninsula.

OBSTRUCTION POINT: A scenic drive with wildflowers, marmots, deer, bear, and mountaintop views leads nine miles east of Hurricane Ridge Lodge to Obstruction Point. The road, called Alpine Drive, is narrow and steep in places but is scheduled for improvement and paving.

OCEAN SHORES: A resort development with motels, restaurants, and shops begun in 1960. There is a public clam beach; also bass, perch, and sole fishing, and duck and geese hunting.

OCEAN CITY: West of Aberdeen-Hoquiam, this is one of the beach resort towns along the Peninsula's famed razor clam beaches, where three hundred thousand people each year dig their limits. Notice the public clam-cleaning sinks and the shops advertising custom cleaning, packaging, canning, or smoking of clams. Ample accommodations and supplies; state park south of town.

OLYMPIA: Two 160-acre homesteads settled in 1846 started Olympia, now the state capital. Six years after the homesteaders planted crops they found a townsite laid out next to their land, and in another four years carpenters started building the first capitol.

The present capitol, a successor to the original building, was completed in 1935. Guides conduct tours daily and at midday there is a free organ recital in the rotunda. The State Historical Museum, originally a private mansion, houses Northwest displays and art exhibits; the Crosby Mansion, built by Bing Crosby's grandfather in the 1860's, is open by appointment. Several industrial plants offer tours: Georgia Pacific Corrugated Container Company, on Fones Road; the Merchant Marine Reserve Fleet, on Budd Inlet north of downtown Olympia; Olympia Brewing Company, south of town on US 99; Olympia Cheese Company, Martin Way; St. Paul and Tacoma Plywood, downtown Olympia; and Weyerhaeuser Mills, on Union Mills Road.

OLYMPIC HOT SPRINGS: A resort used to be operated at these springs, in a forested side canyon above the Elwha Valley. Plans now are to dismantle the lodge and restore the hot springs to their natural condition.

OLYMPIC NATIONAL FOREST: National forests are managed for economic productivity—logging, grazing, and mining—watershed and wildlife protection, and public recreation. In Olympic National Forest about two hundred twenty million board feet of timber are harvested each year, and about two million trees are planted to provide for the future. Back-country roads are generally open to the public but are intended primarily as work roads rather than for sightseeing. The main through-roads, scenic

PARK RANGER-NATURALIST TALK, HURRICANE RIDGE

points, and campgrounds in Olympic National Forest are listed in the Directory.

OLYMPIC NATIONAL PARK: Snowy peaks, alpine meadows, rain forests, and wilderness beaches distinguish Olympic from all other national parks. It was formally dedicated in 1946 after a series of efforts to assure preservation of its scenic and scientific features. US 101 circles the Park but touches its borders only at Lake Crescent and Kalaloch; ten roads lead up the valleys but none cut through the mountains. To sample the highlights of Olympic National Park visit Hurricane Ridge, the Hoh Rain Forest, and the beaches at LaPush or Rialto.

All national parks are retained in their natural state, with landscape unaltered and plants and animals undisturbed: areas set aside from the commercial mainstream of the nation because of special aesthetic and cultural value.

Picnic areas, campgrounds, and trails are listed in the Directory. Major points of interest are included alphabetically in this section. Museums are at Port Angeles, Lake Crescent, and Hoh Rain Forest. The area of the Park is 1,400 square miles.

OYSTER BAY: Coves between Olympia and Shelton produce three hundred thousand gallons of Pacific oysters each year and six thousand gallons of the tiny native Olympia oysters, the smallest oyster in the world. At maturity the shell of this species is no bigger than a silver dollar, and the meat of five hundred fit in a quart jar. For a tour of an oyster-processing plant visit the Olympia Oyster Company, on Oyster Bay, south of Shelton.

PACIFIC BEACH: Northwest of Hoquiam-Aberdeen this is a resort town fine for relaxing, clam digging, or beach combing. Ample supplies and services for basic tourist needs. The U.S. Naval Facility is engaged in oceanographic research largely of a classified nature; not open to the public.

POINT OF ARCHES: The approach road, south of Neah Bay, varies from passable to hopeless—appropriate, somehow, for a last wild headland where bald eagles nest in weathered snags and the surf pounds ceaselessly at the offshore rock, wearing the arches even larger. The rocks are the children of Destruction Island and Tatoosh Island, according to legend; and they are here because when Tatoosh deserted her husband she pushed them out of her canoe, saying, "You'd probably grow up just like your father!"

North of Point of Arches is Shi-Shi Beach, ideal for strolling and beach combing. North of it is Portage Head, with a sea cave at its base and viewpoints and World War II bunkers high on its cliff. Experienced drivers usually can negotiate the road as far as Portage Head; from there the way is by foot on the beach. A road is proposed from Portage Head south to Lake Ozette.

PORT ANGELES: In 1791 the Spanish explorer Francisco Eliza rounded the tip of a long sandspit and named the bay it forms *Porto de Nuestra Señora de Los Angeles,* Port of Our Lady of the Angels. Seventy-one years later Abraham Lincoln set aside land on the bay for "lighthouse and military purposes" and the government laid out a townsite, the first after Washington, D.C., to be federally planned. At the time, the total population was exactly ten.

In 1887 settlers landed just east of the federal townsite and founded the Puget Sound Cooperative Colony, a try at communal living. Their charter stipulated the "emancipation of women from the slavery of domestic drudgery" and that "everyone shall act as a civilized being." Property

POINT OF ARCHES

FISHING FLEET, PORT ANGELES

was owned in common; the work load evenly shared without compensation. But Utopia failed to result. After seven years, hope surrendered to realism and the colony went into receivership. But Port Angeles endured. In 1891 the federal townsite was opened to settlers, and today it is the logging center of the north Peninsula, cutting four hundred million board feet of timber each year and turning it into lumber, plywood, fiberboard, newsprint, and chemical cellulose. To see the process, visit the Crown Zellerbach papermill, the Peninsula Plywood mill, the Rayonier cellulose mill. These three offer scheduled tours the year round.

For a view of Port Angeles from across the harbor, drive onto Ediz Hook, the sandspit fingering three miles into the Strait. Try it at dusk when sea gulls are settling on the log booms, and the city lights dance on the water backdropped by the silhouette of the Olympics. The Pilot Station at the end of the public road dispatches a pilot to every passing ship of foreign or United States registry. He advises the captain regarding Puget Sound channels, currents, and tides. The Coast Guard station at the end of the Hook is the only federal land remaining from Lincoln's decree. It is an air station employing helicopters and fixed-wing craft for rescues and patrols and is open to the public on weekends and holidays.

Port Angeles offers ample accommodations, supplies, and services. Its resident population is under fifteen thousand, but in summer it sleeps an additional overnight population of seven thousand.

PORT GAMBLE: Pope and Talbot, a Maine timber company, started a saw screaming through logs here in 1858, and a house built the following year is believed to be the oldest extant in the state. Clipper ships, schooners, and barks from all over the world loaded lumber at the Port Gamble docks. A specialty was spars for the navies of Spain, France, and England.

The docks still groan under the weight of lumber and the white-steepled church and high-roofed houses of the old town show its New England background. But the hustle of the frontier is gone and the quiet prevails.

North of Port Gamble is Point No Point, a lonely spot marked only by a blinking navigation light, the site where the treaty was signed with the Indians in 1855. Here two eras met and dropped the curtain on the old days of canoes and potlatches, and raised it on the new days of roads and commerce.

PORT LUDLOW: Log booms rise and fall with the tide at old Ludlow, near the north end of Hood Canal, and a leftover concrete powerhouse lends an imposing air to the sandspit; but the smell of sawdust is gone. In 1878 a second Pope and Talbot sawmill started here, a complement to the parent mill at nearby Port Gamble. Cyrus Walker, in charge of the operation, lived in a glittering three-story mansion with a thirty-eight-star United States flag fluttering from its roof and a cannon beside its porch to roar salutes at foreign ships coming for lumber.

Today ivy climbs the elms and maples brought around Cape Horn as slips for the Walkers' garden; and the mill is gone, burned purposely because it had become a hazard. The only "Port Ludlow" with life instead of history and a view, is a crossroads community one mile north of the defunct, original Ludlow. When the mill closed, the post office moved to the nearest inhabited community and kept the old name. No tourist facilities are in either the old or the new Port Ludlow except a post office and store. The drives to Mats-Mats and Olele Point are not as scenic as they appear on the map because trees hide the water; the same is true of the Oak Bay drive to Hadlock, north of Port Ludlow.

PORT TOWNSEND: The tip of the Olympic Peninsula, where the Strait merges with Puget Sound, seems an unlikely spot for a dynamic urban center. But during the 1870's and 1880's Port Townsend was one of the most glittering cities on the West Coast. Brick buildings turned the filled-in tideflats into a thriving business center, and lavish homes graced the bluffs above the bay. French mansard roofs, four-story gabled cupolas, stained glass windows, muraled ceilings—these were standard architecture and decor. By 1889 only New York's harbor could boast more than the num-

VICTORIAN MANSION, PORT TOWNSEND

ber of ships tying up in Port Townsend. Then fate reversed itself. Seattle and Tacoma grew as shipping centers, and Port Townsend languished. The financial panic of 1893 hit hard. Life in the mansions was over.

Architectural historians rate Port Townsend as the finest representative of the Victorian era north of San Francisco. The Rothschild house, managed by the State Parks Commission, is open to the public, as is the art gallery portion of the Bartlett house. A museum exhibits heirlooms and documents of the town's glory days, and with deliberate relish its rooms are just one floor above the old county jail which for two nights housed Jack London, the famed author.

South of town is the site of Old Fort Townsend, established in 1856 and utilized until World War II. It now is a state historical park. Nearby is a Crown Zellerbach paper mill, which offers tours of the entire process of making paper bags, from logs floating in the mill pond to bags ready for shipment to grocery stores. Tourist accommodations and supplies are available in Port Townsend.

QUEETS RAIN FOREST: Seven miles south of the US 101 Queets bridge a road turns into the rain forest and follows upriver into Olympic National Park. It passes through stands of spruce, hemlock, and redcedar and crosses flats with maples made shaggy by epiphytic clubmosses and lichens. As many as one hundred species may grow on a single bigleaf maple tree. The Queets River is only thirty miles long, from its beginning in the glaciers to its ending in the surf; but notice its great flow. Rain forest rivers in the Olympics characteristically are short, but full size in terms of volume.

Watch from the US 101 bridge for Indians pulling salmon into their canoes from gill nets set in the river.

QUILCENE: The main supply center on US 101 between Hoodsport and Sequim is Quilcene. On the north edge of town notice the brush-packing warehouse, a forest industry typical of the Peninsula. Brush pickers gather sword fern, salal, and evergreen huckleberry, working under contract, and packers ship the greenery to florists throughout the country the year round.

The Linger Longer Road along the east shore of Quilcene Bay south of town is a pleasant tidelands drive past log booming grounds and oyster houses. The Toandos Peninsula road is too treelined to permit either water or mountain views.

QUINAULT RAIN FOREST: The full beauty of a forest cannot be sensed from a moving car, but the Quinault forest is particularly striking even for a motorist. Spruce and hemlock tower overhead; clubmoss and lichen drape the branches of maple trees; sword fern turns the floor into chest-high green. Bands of elk are frequent, especially in fall. A Forest Service nature trail threads through a beautiful grove of trees near the Quinault Ranger Station, about a mile off US 101. The trail to Enchanted Valley leaves from the end of the East Fork Quinault road. For a view of a narrow gorge luxuriant with maidenhair fern, walk this trail for about a half-mile, to the first bridge.

RIALTO BEACH: Off US 101 west of Forks, this beach is part sand and part covered with round, water-polished stones which delight both eye and touch. Walk south along the sandspit for a view of LaPush across the Quillayute River, and at low tide for access to James Island without wading. Walk north about a mile for a sea tunnel and a reef with outstanding tidepools. Ranger-naturalists lead beach walks in summer. No accommodations other than National Park picnic grounds and a campground nearby at Mora.

RUBY BEACH: A sand beach twenty-seven miles south of Forks on US 101; seastacks, driftwood, and a creek. No accommodations, but in their stead the enticement of sea arches to explore and wild beauty to contemplate.

SAPPHO: Here is a logging town built mostly of "skid houses" belonging to the era when companies moved their men's homes from one logging operation to the next instead of daily transporting the men into the woods and leaving the houses in an established camp. Long, narrow proportions allowed houses to be put on skids and dragged, at first by oxen, later on the bed of a truck. Most homes in Sappho are built of two or three skid houses joined together for added roominess.

SMELTING, RUBY BEACH

A major highway intersection is at the west edge of the town—the beginning of the Burnt Mountain Road connecting US 101 and State 112. The town's name comes from the Greek poetess, Sappho; the loveliness of the forest suggested her to the first settlers, a Kansas family which arrived in 1889. Gasoline and restaurant in Sappho; no other tourist facilities.

SEKIU: So many boats ride the swells off Sekiu when the salmon are running that the whole bay is freckled with bobbing spots. King and silver salmon feed here by the thousands, the first major feeding ground on their migration from ocean to home river.

Below the highway just east of town men scale railway carloads of logs for species and board feet, and the logs then are dumped into the bay sending up great splashes of white foam. Next, "boom" boats and men with long-handled "pike poles" work them into high "Davis rafts" for tugboats to tow to Rayonier mills. The whole process, from dumping to rafting, is called "booming."

SEKIU BOOMING GROUND

Sekiu (pronounced *See-kee-u*) is reached via State 112 west of Port Angeles. It is a sports fishing center with cabins; gasoline, groceries, and boats are available.

SEQUIM: For proof that it doesn't always rain in the Olympics go to Sequim, on US 101 near the northeast tip of the Peninsula. Rainfall there averages sixteen inches per year, only an inch and a half more than in Los Angeles, California. In summer the sun shines sixty-five per cent of the daylight hours, the same percentage as in Miami, Florida. Yet only forty miles from Sequim, straight line, the Hoh Valley has ten times as much rain and three times as many cloudy days. This is because clouds sweeping in from the Pacific cool as they rise above the mountains and their moisture condenses and falls before they get inland as far as the northeast Peninsula. In Sequim farmers irrigate their pastures and many of the plants in the mountains behind town are xerophytes, plants typical of the desert.

Sequim has been an agricultural supply center since early settlement days. Its mild climate and bucolic charm now make it also a retirement center. The name is pronounced *Skwim,* an Anglicized version of the Indian name *Such-e-kwai-ing!* A full range of basic travel needs is available.

On the shores of the Strait four miles north of Sequim, at Jamestown, is the unmarked site of where the Spanish explorer Manuel Quimper beached his longboat one summer day in 1790 and erected a cross to claim the land for Carlos III.

SHELTON: One and one-half million Christmas trees are shipped from Shelton each November and December. The soil is relatively poor, which makes it ideal for Christmas trees because they grow slowly enough for their branches to be closeset and bushy. Growing them is year-round work. Pruning is done in winter; fertilizing to deepen color, in spring; shaping, in summer; harvesting, in fall. The trees, mostly Douglas-fir here, mature to Christmas size in ten or fifteen years whereas to reach sawlog size on this soil, they would require two or three hundred years.

To see a different forest industry, tour the Simpson Timber Company automated mill where in a single hour pushbuttons and ten men can cut enough lumber for an entire house. Saw blades, valued as high as $1,500 each, must be sharpened every three hours.

Accommodations, goods, and services are available in Shelton. Roads radiate from town into the woods, leading into commercial forestland dotted with lakes (some with resorts, some untouched). State 3, northeast of Shelton, leads past log booms which are stranded twice daily when low tide drains Oakland Bay as though it were water going out from a tub.

SOL DUC HOT SPRINGS: A resort and warm-water swimming pool; the

SOLEDUCK VALLEY

springs themselves are not showy, but the drive up the valley is through beautiful forest leaving US 101 just west of Lake Crescent.

From August to October salmon fight up the Soleduck River to spawn. They leap above the torrent of Salmon Cascades, five miles down river from the resort, sometimes gaining the next higher pool and sometimes falling back to try again. Ranger-naturalists give programs through the summer; a nature trail is to be built.

STRAIT OF JUAN DE FUCA: One hundred years after Columbus' voyage a seaman named Juan de Fuca seems to have discovered this coast, "finding . . . a broad Inlet of the Sea and sayling therein more than twentie dayes," to quote a book later published in London.

In 1930, three hundred and thirty-eight years after Juan de Fuca's arrival, State Highway 112 was finished from Port Angeles to Neah Bay, the first road to span the length of the Strait. It is scenic, sometimes above the water with sweeping views, sometimes hugging the beach. It passes two commercial tree farms where trees are planted and harvested on much the same basis as any other crop; and it leads past fishing villages, logging villages, and small ranches set in forest clearings.

TAHOLAH: The general store in Taholah, on the Quinaielt Indian Reservation, gives insight into the life of the community. Notice the tools for mending fishnets, salmon clubs like short baseball bats to kill fish as they are taken from the nets, raffia for the women to use with cedar bark and beargrass in making baskets, especially designed metal frames to hold lanterns while digging clams at night, and bells for Shaker Church services, an Indian-Christian faith that originated on the Peninsula in 1881.

Tribal headquarters are at Taholah. Fishing and hunting guides, required on reservation land, may be arranged here. A beach campground is south of town; otherwise there are no tourist facilities. Three miles south of Taholah is Point Grenville, the site of Bruno Heceta's landing in 1775. Also at Point Grenville is a Coast Guard loran station ("long range aid to navigation"); the grounds are open to the public on weekends and holidays. North of Taholah a road under construction over Cape Elizabeth will join an existing fire patrol road to provide an oceanside link to US 101 at Queets. Ultimately it will be paved.

TONGUE POINT: Located west of Port Angeles via State 112, this spit of land is a fine sunset viewpoint. Notice the midden shell and bone in the soil, mute evidence of long-ago Indian dinners. Bunkers tunneled into the hilltop are Fort Hayden, a World War II installation, now used to house Clallam County emergency supplies. Nearby is Salt Creek Park, a public picnic area and campground. At the base of the cliff are tidepools with hermit crabs, sea cucumbers, anemones, urchins, and other forms of littoral life.

TIDEPOOL LIFE: BARNACLES, MUSSELS, SNAILS

**Part 4
TRAIL GUIDE**

About eight hundred miles of trail lead through the back country of Olympic National Park and Olympic National Forest, threading forest valleys, climbing ridges and peaks, and opening onto wilderness beaches.

Trails in the high country seldom melt free of snow until July, or even August, and staying on a route when the trail is invisible can be difficult for inexperienced hikers. Topographic maps help. They are available at the Olympic National Park headquarters museum in Port Angeles and at most ranger stations; also from the U.S. Geological Survey, Denver, Colorado.

Lowland forests are fine hiking in winter, as well as in summer. The clubmoss draperies on trees are more conspicuous without the screening leaves, and views hidden in summer reappear. Even on wet days a dry spot for lunch usually can be found beneath a spruce. Beaches, too, are suitable for year-round hiking. Always observe tide tables; take no chance of getting caught by rising water while rounding a point.

Trails listed here are recommended as particularly rewarding for the miles and effort involved. The relief model at the National Park museum in Port Angeles is worth studying for a preview of trails. For further suggestions and detailed information, ask a park ranger or a forest ranger.

ANDERSON PASS: The pass is a pleasant meadow atop the divide between the Dosewallips and Quinault drainages. Just above it is the most easily reached glacier in the Park, one replete with classic crevasses, moraines, and icebergs floating in its meltpond. Nearby are many aquamarine tarns and panoramic mountain views. Bands of elk are frequent. *Trail:* Along the Dosewallips River; wooded and gentle grade practically to Anderson Pass, 9.1 miles. A steep scramble up heather slopes leads from the pass to the moraine above Anderson Glacier. Adequate equipment and experience are needed for venturing onto the ice, but the moraine is safe. Recommended as a hike from one side of the Olympics through to the other, if transportation can be arranged. Equally fine hiked either direction.

BOGACHIEL RIVER: This trail penetrates a heavily forested, pristine valley that is seldom visited. Sitka spruce and western hemlock grow in stilted colonnades, their buttresses blanketed by foamflower, woodsorrel, and bedstraw. Fine chance of seeing elk, deer, bear, and otter. *Trail:* Reached by a rough road turning off US 101 just north of the Bogachiel bridge.

79

The road is about 3 miles long but the drivable length depends on current washouts and bogs. The trail follows the river; gentle grades. If time and transportation permit, the trail can be hiked through Slide Pass to Little Divide and down to the Soleduck River via Deer Lake, a total distance of 24.1 miles.

BOULDER LAKE: Flowers and alpine fir ring the lake and Boulder Peak rises abruptly above it. Notice the burls swelling the trunks of trees along the trail on the way in. *Trail:* 3.4 miles from Olympic Hot Springs to the lake, in the trees almost all the way.

CAPE ALAVA–SAND POINT: There are more features of interest per mile here than along most of the coast. Cape Alava is the westernmost point in conterminous United States. North of where the trail through the forest emerges onto the beach is the site of the Ozette Indian Village (abandoned about fifty years ago) and its canoe dragway, cleared through the rocks of the reef. On the east side of Indian Island, accessible without wading at low tide, are "cannonball" concretions. The anchor of the ship *Austria,* wrecked in 1887, is on the reef and pieces of bulkhead are half buried in the sand. The mouth of the Ozette River is easy to reach but not to cross; too swift and deep. Wedding Rock, north of Sand Point, is covered with petroglyphs, drawings chipped into the rock by Indians. Neither their age nor meaning is known. Yellow Banks, south of Sand Point, can be rounded on a fairly low tide with a sea tunnel furnishing passage the last of the way; it is not feasible to climb due to steep cliffs and tangled underbrush. The cabins on the bluff south of Yellow Banks date from the depression days of the 1930's when panning gold out of the beach sand was a way to eke out a living. *Trail:* From Lake Ozette Ranger Station, 3 miles to the beach; then along the beach 3 miles; and 3 miles back to Ozette by the Sand Point trail: 9 miles total. Equally enjoyable hiked either direction. Trail is practically level with puncheon walkway bridging the wet spots.

DEER LAKE: This is a fair-sized lake just below timberline. Several small lakes and marshes close by; explore around a bit. *Trail:* 4.0 miles from end of Soleduck road to the lake. Almost level for the first mile, to Soleduck Falls, then a steady climb and switchbacks.

DOSE MEADOW: Hikers will enjoy trekking across this beautiful open meadow country surrounded by snow peaks. Especially fine in July when the flowers are at the height of bloom. *Trail:* Follows Dosewallips River, 12.8 miles. Forested until above Camp Marion, 8.3 miles, then flowers, heather, and subalpine fir.

ELWHA RIVER: Douglas-fir and western hemlock cloak the river valley, interspersed with bottoms of alder, maple, and cottonwood. Humes Ranch and Anderson Ranch are homestead sites down in the river bottom below the main trail; some buildings remain. A cougar hunter's homestead cabin is on the main trail about 2½ miles from the road. The Elwha is considered the best river fishing in the park, especially in the Elkhorn to Hayes River vicinity. *Trail:* Leaves the road at Whiskey Bend, a spur off the main Elwha Valley road. Crosses up and over the toes of several side ridges until about Mary's Fall Camp, 8.8 miles; then follows the river fairly closely. Connects with Hayden Pass and over to the Dosewallips, a total of 40.9 miles from the road up the Elwha to the road up the Dosewallips. Also connects with Low Divide and the North Fork of the Quinault River, 44.1 miles from one road to the other.

ENCHANTED VALLEY: This valley is well named. It is a great gorge with sheer rock walls laced by waterfalls: ten or more are visible in a single glance during the heavy June runoff. Mount Anderson and the Hanging Glacier head the valley. A two-story log chalet built as a resort before establishment of the Park now serves as trail shelter. Watch for elk and bear. Mountain goats are often scrambling on the cliffs above the valley. *Trail:* Leads along the Quinault River through exceptionally beautiful alder and cottonwood bottoms; some climbs where side ridges finger into the Quinault, but none is long or steep. 10.9 miles to Enchanted Valley from Graves Creek, end of the road beyond Lake Quinault.

HUMES RANCH

GRAND LAKE

FLAPJACK LAKES–GLADYS DIVIDE: Only a narrow strip of land separates the two Flapjack Lakes. One is shallow and swampy, the other deep and dotted with boulders. Both are surrounded by trees. Gladys Divide is meadow country with sweeping views, lush wildflower fields, and frequent tarns. *Trail:* Leaves from near the end of the road up the North Fork of the Skokomish. 4.1 miles to Flapjacks; 1.5 mile farther to Gladys Divide.

GRAND VALLEY: Grand Lake, Moose Lake, and Upper Lake string along the valley in a manner known geologically as *pater noster* lakes. They mark successive stages in the retreat of the glacier that carved the valley. Watch for marmots near Moose Lake and also in Badger Valley, below Grand Lake. Flowers are at their best in July. *Trail:* Leaves from the end of the road at Obstruction Point and follows along the ridge, then drops into the valley, 3.8 miles. A grind coming back out up bare shale slopes; avoid the heat of midday.

HIGH DIVIDE: Flowers, lakes, Mount Olympus soaring above the Hoh

Valley, the distant shimmer of the ocean make this a mecca for hikers. Good chance to see elk, especially on Mount Appleton and in Cat Creek Basin. Sunset view of Mount Olympus is spectacular. *Trail:* Begins at end of Soleduck road. About 8 miles approached via Deer Lake or via Soleduck Park and Heart Lake. The High Divide trail itself is about 4 miles long, and connects with the Bailey Range trail which contours open slopes for another 4 miles, where it ends abruptly.

HOH RIVER: Enormous trees, thick moss, and lush ferns are characteristics of the trail. This is the most popular rain forest hike in the park, and the usual approach for climbs of Mount Olympus. Watch for elk, and also for heavily browsed sword fern and maple marking their feeding. Good chance of seeing bears—and of being bothered by them at Olympus Shelter, Elk Lake, and Glacier Meadows! Coyotes, bobcats, and cougars are seen occasionally, their tracks, commonly. The Sitka spruce long believed the largest in the world (13'4" in diameter) is 3.5 miles up the trail and the largest red alder in the Olympics (also once thought a world's record, 3'9") is a short way beyond. *Trail:* Begins at the Hoh Ranger Station and follows the river bottom for the first 11 miles, then sidehills to Elk Lake, 14 miles, and Glacier Meadows, 16.6 miles. No really steep, prolonged grinds. Elk Lake usually is good fishing early in the season. Glacier Meadows actually is a wooded glade on upper Glacier Creek, not a meadow. A one-mile trail leads above Glacier Meadows to the moraine above the lower Blue Glacier.

HOH BRIDGE

LAKE CONSTANCE

Only experienced and equipped climbers should go onto the ice, but the moraine is safe. Notice the glacial polish on the rocks near the snout.

LAKE CONSTANCE: This is an exceptionally lovely alpine lake rimmed by towering rock peaks; hikers will have a fine time exploring up the valley above it. Mountain goats are an almost certain sight, perhaps coming right into camp. *Trail:* 2 miles from Dosewallips road to lake—miles that seem straight up!

LENA LAKES: Two lakes, one in the forest, the other in alpine country are the features of this trail. Each is a beautiful representative of its type. Rainbow and eastern brook trout. *Trail:* 2 miles to Lower Lena and 6 miles to upper Lena, from near the end of the Hamma Hamma road. Forested all the way.

MARMOT LAKE–HART LAKE: Here are a succession of high alpine meadows and ridges with lakes and far-flung views. Good chance to see elk and mountain goats between Anderson Pass and O'Neil Pass. *Trail:*

Several approaches. 14.8 miles from Staircase to Marmot Lake with a five-thousand-foot ridge to climb up and over at Home Sweet Home; about 20 miles either up the Duckabush or the Dosewallips via Anderson Pass and O'Neil Pass. Also possible from the Quinault via Enchanted Valley, about 23 miles by the regular trail or with way-trail shortcuts on the south side of Enchanted Valley.

MOUNT ANGELES: Notice here the views first back toward the Olympics, then a sudden view north to Mt. Baker and the Strait as the trail crosses through the Notch on Klahhane Ridge. The trail climbs and dips among the rocky crags of Mount Angeles' three peaks; then drops through the meadows of Heather Park and into the forest. Branch trail to Lake Angeles. Mountain goats are frequent on Klahhane Ridge. *Trail:* 10 miles from Hurricane Ridge to Heart o' the Hills. Snow usually covers the trail below the Notch until August.

NORWEGIAN MEMORIAL: On the wilderness beach north of LaPush stands this memorial commemorating the dead of a 1903 shipwreck. The small points south of the Memorial offer sweeping marine views of surf and seastacks. Watch for whales and bald eagles. *Trail:* The shortest way is

MARMOT LAKE

through the forest 2.3 miles from Allen's Bay, near the south end of Lake Ozette; more frequent approaches are along the beach either south from Sand Point or north from Rialto Beach.

OBSTRUCTION POINT tO DEER PARK: An alpine hike, this has the double pleasure of a marine view northward and a mountain view southward. Look and listen for marmots in Badger Valley, below the trail at the Obstruction Point end. *Trail:* Equally fine hiked west to east, or east to west. The trail undulates along the ridge for 7.6 miles; never steep. Carry water.

ROYAL BASIN: Shelving meadows and a lake nestle directly beneath the Needles and Mount Deception. Chance to explore raw mountain land newly released from ice and still snow-covered most of the year: scree, moraines, tarns. Easy access to peaks and to glaciers. *Trail:* 6.5 miles along Dungeness River and Roy Creek; forested until the last mile. Trailhead reached via Upper Dungeness road about 10 miles above Louella Guard Station (use map or inquire; confusing road junctions).

SEVEN LAKES: This high cirque basin is studded with far more tarns than "seven." In fact one of the lakes is named Number Eight! Most of the slopes and lakes seldom melt free of snow until early August. *Trail:* From the Soleduck road up past Soleduck Falls and Deer Lake, 8.5 miles. Fine loop hike by going on to High Divide and out via Heart Lake and Soleduck Park, about 20 miles.

SKYLINE–KIMTA PEAK: The hike leads from cedar swamps to alpine meadows, with several small lakes along the way. Kimta Peak is the high point of the surrounding country with views of the forbidding south side of Mount Olympus and down into the Queets and Quinault rivers. Elk and bear are likely. *Trail:* Steady climb from the North Fork of the Quinault, 18.7 miles via Three Lakes or 25.3 via Mount Noyes. Open country for 20 miles from Low Divide to Three Lakes. Trail is hard to follow between Lake Beauty and Promise Creek because of bare slopes and snow. Not recommended until late August.

SOUTH HOH: So seldom used is this rain forest trail that solitude is assured. The forest floor underfoot has the virgin springy quality born of centuries of undisturbed growth. *Trail:* Reached via logging roads; inquire current status. The old Huelsdonk Bridge across the Hoh River is gone but a new one is under construction nearby. The trail tends to be overgrown, but experienced hikers follow it with only occasional confusion.

TOLEAK POINT: This low point studded with offshore seastacks lies about midway on the South Wilderness Beach. Beautiful reefs at low tide, and good butter clam digging. Elk and deer sometimes swim or wade to the offshore islands. *Trail:* South from Third Beach near LaPush for 5.5 miles, or north from the Hoh River, 9 miles. From Third Beach to Toleak Point and back is a fine one-day hike, tide permitting.

SOUTH WILDERNESS BEACH

Part 5
DIRECTORY

DIRECTORY

ROADS

Highways loop the Peninsula; both paved and graded roads lead from them into the forest, the mountains, and to the beaches. No road crosses the rugged mountain interior, through Olympic National Park. In Olympic National Forest and on State Department of Natural Resources land, roads are primarily work roads although most are also open to the public. Main roads are well graded and easily traveled most of the time; some are narrow and steep and not recommended for passenger cars. To avoid inconvenience, check with forest rangers or wardens. Logging trucks are to be expected on weekdays; road junctions often are unsigned; locked gates sometimes close portions of roads because of fire danger or active logging operations.

Thoroughfares

US 101 loops the Peninsula: Olympia to Port Angeles to Aberdeen. A slow road along Hood Canal and Lake Crescent, but beautiful; continually goes in and out of Olympic National Forest and Olympic National Park which causes confusion between the two.

US 410 crosses the base of the Peninsula: Olympia to Aberdeen. Fast road.

State 112 leads along the Strait: Port Angeles to Neah Bay. Slow because of curves; close to the water and scenic most of the way.

State 109 connects the beaches north of Grays Harbor: Aberdeen to the Copalis Beach area. New bridge over the Quinault River; road from Taholah to Queets scheduled for completion soon.

Burnt Mountain Road links US 101 and State 112: Sappho to Pysht. Paved; mountainous but recently widened and improved.

Byways to Explore (Unpaved and may be muddy)

Bear Creek Road links US 101 and State 112 west of Lake Crescent. Unpaved but passable the year around; no steep grades. Opportunity to see both the black devastation of forest fire and fine commercial timber.

Bon Jon Pass road crosses Mt. Zion: Sequim to Quilcene. Unpaved; readily negotiable for anyone accustomed to driving back roads; particularly beautiful in June when rhododendrons are blooming.

Skokomish, Hamma Hamma, Duckabush, and *Dosewallips* roads, and the forest access road parallel to US 101 that connects these drainages, are usually passable for experienced drivers. Fine young-growth timber; occasional moldering logging railroad trestles; view of Hood Canal from Webb Lookout. (Road to Lookout is not recommended for passenger cars.)

91

ROAD TO DEER PARK

Blyn Lookout offers a view of the Strait, Hood Canal, the Cascades, and the Olympics. Narrow road; leaves US 101 at tip of Sequim Bay; portion on to Leland via Snow Creek usually closed to public.

Striped Peak, west of Port Angeles, overlooks the Strait and back to the Olympics. Easy road for experienced drivers.

North Point, on the ridge west of Lake Crescent, offers a view from the Pacific near LaPush to the Strait near Port Angeles and into the high Olympics. The road is a steady climb and tends to be rocky.

Hyas Lookout gives a view across the Forks Burn and to the Olympics. Road is steep; connects from Forks to Snider, on the Soleduck River.

Higley Peak, above Lake Quinault, is a vantage point for the lake, the ocean, and the mountains. Gravel road.

Humptulips, Wishkah, Wynoochee, and *Satsop* drainages are threaded by a maze of easily passable roads; some are poorly signed. The scene is a blend of pastoral beauty and productive timberland.

Kitsap Peninsula is crisscrossed with graded roads leading through green tunnels of trees and past lakes; many unsigned junctions. Magnificent views of the Olympics from the Hood Canal side; especially striking when the rhododendrons are in bloom in May and June.

FERRIES

Six automobile ferries cross to the Olympic Peninsula the year around. Those from Seattle, Edmonds, and Fauntleroy offer striking views of the Puget Sound urban skyline to the east and the jagged wilderness of peaks to the west. Try one of these at dusk when the electric glitter of the cities contrasts sharply with the black openness of water and forest and mountains. The ferries from Whidbey Island and Victoria, B.C., show the Olympic Mountains to particular advantage. They rise from the sea as abruptly as cardboard cutouts, with Port Townsend and Port Angeles scaled like model towns at their base. Whales and seals are seen sometimes, on all routes; fishing boats and tugs towing log booms are usual sights. The ferries are worth considering as excursions even without taking the car (to reduce cost). Check with Washington State Ferries for schedules.

Seattle to Bremerton: 1 hour. Downtown Seattle to downtown Bremerton.

Seattle to Winslow: 35 minutes. Downtown Seattle to Bainbridge Island; then via Agate Pass and Hood Canal bridges to the Olympic Peninsula.

Edmonds to Kingston: 30 minutes. Edmonds is just north of Seattle; Kingston is on the Kitsap Peninsula east of Hood Canal Bridge.

Fauntleroy–Vashon Island–Southworth: 30 minutes. Fauntleroy is just south of Seattle; Southworth is east of Bremerton.

Keystone to Port Townsend: 35 minutes. Crosses from the south tip of Whidbey Island to Port Townsend, northeast tip of the Olympic Peninsula.

Victoria, B.C., to Port Angeles: 1 hour 15 minutes. From the harbor in downtown Victoria to Port Angeles, largest town on northern Olympic Peninsula.

OLYMPIC PENINSULA FERRY

PUBLIC TRANSPORTATION

The Peninsula's combination of wilderness and industry is reflected in its transportation services: they range from dugout canoes and pack trains to buses and airplanes.

Bus

Greyhound from Seattle to Port Angeles: 3-hour trip, several times daily.

Greyhound from Seattle or Portland to Olympia and Aberdeen: 2-hour trip Seattle to Olympia, 2 hours Portland to Olympia, 1¼ hours Olympia to Aberdeen, several times daily.

Local bus between Port Angeles, Forks, and Neah Bay: Daily, inquire at Greyhound Depot, Port Angeles.

Local bus in Grays Harbor area: Daily, inquire at Greyhound Depot, Aberdeen.

Greyline Tours out from Port Angeles: Various schedules and destinations in summer; weekend service to Hurricane Ridge in ski season.

Airplanes

West Coast Airlines

    Seattle to Port Angeles: 35 minutes, daily.

    Seattle to Olympia: 23 minutes, daily.

    Seattle to Aberdeen: 42 minutes, daily.

    Portland to Olympia: 45 minutes, daily.

    Portland to Aberdeen: 1 hour 10 minutes, daily.

Charter Plane

    Port Angeles: scenic flights and through transportation.

U-Drive cars

    Olympia, Bremerton, Port Angeles, Aberdeen.

Pack Trips and Burros

    Inquire for current services: Olympic National Park Headquarters, Port Angeles, and Olympic National Forest district ranger stations.

Dugout Canoe

    Somewhat irregular service on Quinault River between Amanda Park and Taholah; inquire general store in Amanda Park or Lake Quinault Lodge. Individual arrangements for trips often are possible in LaPush and Taholah.

LODGING

Motels, resorts, and fishing camps dot the lowlands of the Peninsula and offer accommodations from the rustic to the plush. There are no overnight accommodations in the high mountains; the lodge at Hurricane Ridge provides meal service only. For current information write the Olympic Peninsula Resort and Hotel Association or any of the Chambers of Commerce listed among the Sources of Information. Advance reservations are advisable during the summer season, mid-June to mid-September.

TRAILER PARKS

A variety of accommodation is available at commercial trailer parks; consult the Olympic Peninsula Resort and Hotel Association or local Chambers of Commerce listed among the Sources of Information. Some public campgrounds in the list have trailer hookups; trailers are also permitted in the other campgrounds except where road conditions make them inadvisable.

BOAT MOORAGES

A list of commercial boat moorages, both salt water and fresh water, is available from the Department of Commerce and Economic Development; see Sources of Information for address. Public dock tie-ups are operated at the following salt-water state parks: Ft. Flagler, near Port Townsend; Geralds Cove, east of Shelton; Illahee, near Bremerton; Penrose Point, south of Bremerton; Pleasant Harbor, south of Quilcene; Sequim Bay, east of Port Angeles; Twanoh, north of Shelton.

BOAT LAUNCH RAMPS

Commercial ramps are listed in a leaflet available from the Department of Commerce and Economic Development; for address, check Sources of Information. Public ramps are indicated on maps.

SUPPLIES AND SERVICES

Aberdeen, Bremerton, Hoquiam, Olympia, Port Angeles, and Shelton are the main population centers where a full range of travelers' supplies and services may be expected. Some communities shown on maps are very small; advance planning for gasoline and other needs is advisable.

SELF-SERVICE LAUNDRIES

Aberdeen, Bremerton, Clallam Bay, Forks, Hoodsport, Hoquiam, Neah Bay, Ocean Shores, Olympia, Pacific Beach, Port Angeles, Port Townsend, Sequim, Shelton.

ICE

Aberdeen, Bremerton, Copalis Beach, Forks, Hoodsport, Hoquiam, LaPush, Nob Hill (near Sekiu), Olympia, Port Angeles, Sequim, Shelton.

CUSTOM CANNING AND SMOKING OF FISH

Aberdeen, Clallam Bay, Forks, Hoquiam, LaPush, Port Angeles, Westport.

PICNIC AREAS

Try Hurricane Ridge or Mount Walker for a mountain picnic with a panoramic view, or along Hood Canal or Lake Crescent for a water view. Some sites listed are very small, having only one or two tables; many are expanding as demand increases. Most have fireplaces; all have tables, toilets, and water unless otherwise specified—or unless conditions have changed. Campgrounds are also open for picnicking. If it is raining, check the list for a site with a cooking shelter.

Order of listing is alphabetical; maps indicate locations. Elevations of 1,000 feet or more are indicated.

AGATE PENINSULA COUNTY PARK: E across Oakland Bay from Shelton. Cooking shelter.

CHETZEMOKA CITY PARK: In Port Townsend on bluff above the Strait. Cooking shelter, playground.

CHIMACUM COUNTY PARK: 10 mi. S of Port Townsend on county road. Cooking shelter.

COUNTY LINE ROADSIDE REST AREA: 12 mi. N of Olympia. State Department of Highways land. Water view. Carry water; no toilets.

DISCOVERY BAY ROADSIDE REST AREA: 12 mi. E of Sequim on US 101. State Department of Highways land. Historical marker. Carry water; no toilets.

EAST BEACH COUNTY PARK: Marrowstone Island, ½ mi. E of highway, near Nordland. Beach access, boating. Cooking shelter.

EAST QUILCENE ROADSIDE REST AREA: 2 mi. E of Quilcene. State Department of Highways land. Waterfront. Carry water; no toilets.

EDIZ HOOK: On the sandspit protecting the Port Angeles harbor. Lions Club civic project. Sand beach, driftwood, boating.

EVERGREEN CITY PARK: In Bremerton, on saltwater. Tables, playground.

FORKS CITY PARK: N edge of town, on US 101. Open field.

FORT WARD STATE PARK: 5 mi. S of Winslow, not far from ferry. Being developed.

GIG HARBOR CITY PARK: 5 mi. N of Narrows Bridge. Cooking shelter.

HARPER COUNTY PARK: 15 mi. E of Bremerton on State 16 near Harper Ferry terminal. Overlooks Puget Sound. Cooking shelter; no toilets.

HICKS COUNTY PARK: 2½ mi. from W end of Hood Canal Bridge, off US 101 near Shine. Boating. Carry water; no toilets.

HURRICANE RIDGE: 19 mi. S of Port Angeles. National Park. Open ridge with panoramic view of Olympic Mts. Spectacular. Hiking, nature trail nearby, ranger-naturalist talks and walks nearby. Elevation 5,225 feet.

KINGSTON COUNTY PARK: In Kingston near ferry terminal. Old school grounds. Carry water; no toilets.

LA POEL: On Lake Crescent 25 mi. W of Port Angeles via US 101. National Park. In trees by lakeside. Cooking shelter.

LAKE ABERDEEN PARK: 5 mi. E of Aberdeen and N on US 410. On shore of a reservoir. Swimming, boating.

LAKE CRESCENT ROADSIDE PICNIC TABLES: Several turnouts off US 101 along shores of Lake. State Department of Highways. Carry water; no toilets.

LINCOLN CITY PARK: E side of Port Angeles on State 112. Wooded. Cooking shelters, playground, fair ground.

LIONS CITY PARK: In Hoquiam, W side of town. No toilets.

MT. WALKER SUMMIT: 5 mi. S of Quilcene on US 101, then 5 mi. E up mountain road. National Forest. Sweeping view of Puget Sound, Cascades, and Olympics. Fire lookout. Elevation 3,018 feet. Leave trailers before starting up.

NAHWATZEL LAKE: 13 mi. W of Shelton. Lowland lake with forested shores. Boating, picnicking.

NORTH POINT OVERLOOK: 7 mi. E of Sappho on US 101, then 13 mi. up steep road. National Forest. Marine and mountain views. Lookout. Trail to be built to Mt. Muller. Area not yet developed; carry water; no toilets. Elevation 3,340 feet.

OAK BAY COUNTY PARK: 11 mi. S of Port Townsend on the Port Ludlow road. On salt water. Boating, clamming. Cooking shelter; carry water.

POINT ROBINSON COUNTY PARK: Easternmost point of Vashon Island. Not developed; carry water; no toilets.

PORT WILLIAMS (Marlyn Nelson Memorial County Park): 3 mi. NE of Sequim on county road. On the Strait. Rocky beach; boating. Carry water.

PRIEST POINT CITY PARK: N side of Olympia on E Bay Dr. Overlooks inlet with views of Olympic Mts. Hiking, beach, playground.

PURDY CANYON: 7 mi. N of Shelton off US 101. State Department of Highways. Shaded. Cooking shelter.

QUILCENE COUNTY PARK: S edge of Quilcene. In a grove of trees. Cooking shelter.

RIALTO BEACH: 2 mi. N of Forks on US 101, then 13 mi. W. National Park. Over the drift logs from the beach itself; partly open, partly shaded. Beach hiking, ranger-naturalist walks, smelting.

ROADSIDE REST AREAS: 6 and 8 mi. N of Hoodsport. State Department of Highways land. Turnouts with glimpses of Hood Canal below, through the trees. Carry water; no toilets.

ROADSIDE REST AREA: 8 mi. S of Quilcene on U.S. 101. State Department of Highways land. View across Hood Canal. Carry water; no toilets.

SHELTON ROADSIDE PARK: 3½ mi. N of Shelton on US 101 near airport. State Department of Highways. Forested.

TUMWATER FALLS: S side of Olympia on US 99. Land donated by Olympia Brewing Co. Sylvan setting. Hiking along Deschutes River, fish ladder, historic displays including nearby Crosby home.

WALKER COUNTY PARK: 3 mi. E of Shelton on Arcadia Point road. Overlooks Hammersley Inlet; forested. Cooking shelter, playground, salt-water beach.

WATERHOLE: E of Hurricane Ridge on Alpine Drive. National Park. Mountain view, flower meadows, wildlife. Elevation 5,000 feet.

CAMPGROUNDS

Camp on the beach, in the forest, or in the mountains; join with a thousand others, or be alone. Facilities on the Olympic Peninsula vary from the highly developed, replete with children's playgrounds and hot showers, to scarcely touched wilderness accessible by muddy, rutted roads. All sites listed are public; a small fee is charged at state parks and the better federal campgrounds. Many private campgrounds along Hood Canal and the Strait offer beachside camping; ask locally or write in advance. (See Sources of Information for addresses.) Campgrounds with evening campfire programs are: Elwha, Fairholm, Heart O' the Hills, Hoh, Kalaloch, Mora, and Soleduck. Those with trailer hookups are: Dosewallips, Kitsap Memorial, Merrill–Ring, Millersylvania, Ocean City, Potlatch, Schafer, Sequim Bay, Twanoh, Twin Harbors; also privately owned trailer parks. Ask locally or write for current information.

Order of listing is alphabetical; check the maps for locations. Elevations of 1,000 feet or more are indicated.

ALDRICH LAKE: 32 mi. SW of Bremerton, near Dewatto. State Department of Natural Resources land. Close to lake; view of Hood Canal and Olympic Mts. Old logging flume nearby: ½-mile, seven-second chute from log pond to tidewater! 6 sites; minimum development. Get fire permit.

ALTAIRE: 9 mi. W of Port Angeles on US 101, then 4½ mi. S on Elwha River Road. National Park. Among trees along banks of river. Fishing, hiking. 29 sites; not recommended for large trailers.

BELFAIR STATE PARK: 15 mi. SW of Bremerton on State 300. Overlooks Hood Canal; partially wooded. Cooking shelters with gas stoves, hot showers, playground, sand beach, swimming (lifeguard in summer), shallow beginners' pool, salt-water and lake fishing nearby. 150 overnight sites plus picnic tables.

BIG CREEK: 8 mi. NW of Hoodsport on Lake Cushman road. National Forest. Being developed; 60 sites planned.

BIG QUIL RIVER: 2 mi. S of Quilcene on US 101, then 5 mi. NW on Townsend Creek road. National Forest. Forest setting. Stream fishing. 4 sites; not recommended for trailers. Elevation 1,700 feet.

BOB CAMP: N of Hoodsport on Upper Lilliwaup Creek, 2 mi. NE of Lake Cushman road. State Department of Natural Resources land. 2 sites; minimum development. Get fire permit.

BOGACHIEL STATE PARK: 6 mi. S of Forks on US 101. Forested riverbank. Cooking shelter, showers, swings, river fishing. 50 sites.

BROWN CREEK: 9 mi. N of Shelton on US 101, then 20 mi. NW via logging roads. National Forest. On South Fork of Skokomish. Fishing. 6 sites; minimum development.

CAMP CORRELL: 10 mi. W of Bremerton on Gold Creek road. State Department of Natural Resources land. Creekside; young fir and alder. Fishing, hiking. Lake Tahuya nearby (about 2 mi.). 2 sites.

CAMPBELL TREE GROVE: 3 mi. N of Humptulips on US 101, then 27 mi. almost to end of Humptulips River road. Huge fir trees, moss-covered boulders. Fishing. 30 sites.

CAMP RICKEY: 14 mi. SW of Bremerton, then 8 mi. N on county roads. State Department of Natural Resources land. Young growth timber; access to Twin Lake. 5 sites.

CAMP SPILLMAN: 14 mi. SW of Bremerton, then 6 mi. N on county roads. State Department of Natural Resources land. Dougas-fir and cottonwood grove on Tahuya River. 12 sites.

CLALLAM RIVER: 1½ mi. S of Clallam Bay just off State 112. State Department of Natural Resources land. Along forested streambank. Fishing. 3 sites.

COLLINS: 17 mi. S of Quilcene on US 101, then 5 mi. W on Duckabush road. National Forest. Wooded flat along river, secluded. Fishing. 17 sites.

COPPER MINE BOTTOM: 12 mi. N of Queets on Clearwater-Snahapish road. State Department of Natural Resources land. Sword fern and alder bottom. 20 sites; minimum development.

DEEP CREEK: 33 mi. W of Port Angeles, just off State 112. Private land; camping permitted. Open sand flat where creek empties into Strait. Fishing. Undeveloped.

DEER PARK: 6 mi. E of Port Angeles on US 101, then 17 mi. S to end of Blue Mt. road. National Park. Alpine meadow; spectacular views. 2 small shelters; hiking. 10 sites; not recommended for trailers. Elevation 5,400 feet.

DOSEWALLIPS (Muscott Flat): 10 mi. S of Quilcene on US 101, then 15½ mi. W up the Dosewallips. National Park. Setting of tall trees and rushing water. River fishing, hiking. 33 sites; not recommended for trailers. Elevation 1,640 feet.

DOSEWALLIPS STATE PARK: 14 mi. S of Quilcene on US 101. Open grassy delta of Dosewallips River, beside Hood Canal. Fishing, clam digging, oyster picking. 116 sites; trailer hookups.

DUNGENESS FORKS: 13 mi. S of Sequim via Palo Alto road and Louella Guard Station. National Forest. Forest and river setting. Cooking shelter. river fishing. 14 sites; difficult for trailers.

DUNGENESS BAY and STATE PARK: 4 mi. NW of Sequim, just off the Dungeness Marine Dr. At edge of bay, beneath bluff. Camping permitted on county land, but scant development. Picnicking and camping also in state park on spit across the bay, accessible by boat; minimum development.

EAST CROSSING: 4 mi. E of Sequim, then 10 mi. S along Dungeness. National Forest. Deep in a valley; forested. Fishing. 9 sites; not recommended for trailers. In process of development.

ELKHORN: 10 mi. S. of Quilcene on US 101, then 10 mi. W along Dosewallips River. National Forest. Forested, riverside setting. Fishing. 24 sites; to be rebuilt.

ELWHA: 9 mi. W of Port Angeles on US 101, then 3 mi. S on Elwha River road. National Park. Forested river bottom. Cooking shelter, campfire program in summer, river fishing. 23 sites; not recommended for large trailers.

FAIRHOLM: W end of Lake Crescent, 28 mi. W of Port Angeles on US 101. National Park. In maple grove at lakeshore. Campfire program in summer, boating, fishing. 90 sites.

FALLS CREEK: 3 mi. E along S shore of Lake Quinault. National Forest. Forested lakeshore; boat launching. Lake fishing subject to Quinaielt Indian tribal regulation; special license; inquire locally. 26 sites, cooking shelter.

FALLS VIEW: 5 mi. S of Quilcene on US 101. National Forest. Overlooking Quilcene River. 30 sites.

FAY BAINBRIDGE STATE PARK: 7 mi. N of Winslow, not far from ferry. Cooking shelters, boating. 27 sites.

FORT FLAGLER STATE PARK: N tip of Marrowstone Island, accessible by bridges, 18 mi. SE of Port Townsend. Abandoned coastal defense installations. Beachfront for 5½ miles; sweeping views of Cascades and Olympics. Boating, swimming, beach hiking, salt-water fishing from shore and dock. 40 sites.

FOSSEN LAKE: 9 mi. N of Hoodsport off Eagle Creek forest road. State Department of Natural Resources land. 3 sites; minimum development. Get fire permit.

GRAVES CREEK: 42 mi. N of Hoquiam on US 101, then 19 E beyond end of Lake Quinault. National Park. Forested riverbank. Hiking, fishing, 45 sites; not recommended for large trailers.

GREEN MOUNTAIN: 14 mi. W of Bremerton. State Department of Natural Resources fire lookout. View of Puget Sound. 3 sites; minimum development. Get fire permit. Elevation 1,710 feet.

HAMMA HAMMA: 14 mi. N of Hoodsport on US 101, then 6 mi. W. National Forest. Valley bottom. Stream fishing. 17 sites; to be rebuilt.

HAVEN LAKE COUNTY PARK: 15 mi. SW of Bremerton on State 300, then 9 mi. NW. Waterfront access, fishing. 4 sites; not recommended for trailers.

HEART O' THE HILLS: 7 mi. S of Port Angeles on road to Hurricane Ridge. National Park. Forested. Campfire program in summer, scenic drive nearby. 100 sites. Elevation 1,850 feet.

HOH: 14 mi. S of Forks, then 19 mi. E to end of road. National Park. Rain forest along banks of glacier-fed river. Museum, campfire program, and ranger-naturalist walks in summer; nature trails, hiking, river fishing. 100 sites.

HUELSDONK BRIDGE: 12 mi. from US 101 on Upper Hoh Road. State Department of Natural Resources land. Rain forest; riverbank. Minimum development.

ILLAHEE STATE PARK: 3½ mi. NE of Bremerton, via county road. On Sinclair Inlet. Cooking shelters (one with gas stoves), cold showers, ball field, playground, boating, sand beach, swimming, fishing, clamming (rather poor). 50 campsites plus picnic tables.

JULY CREEK: 46 mi. N. of Hoquiam on US 101, then 4 mi. E along N shore of Lake Quinault. National Park. Lakeshore, secluded. Fishing in lake subject to Quinaielt Tribal Council regulation; special license (ask at ranger station or store). 30 walk-in sites; trailers not recommended.

KALALOCH: 34 mi. S of Forks on US 101. National Park. Coastal spruce and cedar forest on bluff above beach. Campfire program and ranger-naturalist walks in summer, clamming, surf fishing, smelting, beach hiking. 170 sites.

KIAHANIE: 2 mi. N of Forks on US 101, then 5 mi. E on Calawah River road. National Forest. Forested riverbank. Being developed; 60 sites planned.

KINGS BOTTOM: 6 mi. NE of US 101 on Queets road. National Park. Open riverbank. Undeveloped.

KITSAP MEMORIAL STATE PARK: 20 mi. N of Bremerton, W of State 3.

Tideland with view across Hood Canal to Olympic Mts.; grassy and wooded. Cooking shelters including gas stoves, ball field, swings, swimming, clamming. 42 sites; trailer hookups.

KLAHOWYA: 35 mi. W of Port Angeles, just off US 101. National Forest. Secluded forest setting along Soleduck River. Nature trail being developed. fishing. 50 sites.

KOPACHUCK STATE PARK: 5 mi. W of Gig Harbor. Cooking shelters, salt-water fishing, clamming, swimming. 84 sites.

LAKE CUSHMAN STATE PARK: 9 mi. NW of Hoodsport. Forested lakeshore. Cooking shelter, hiking, swimming, boating, fishing. 81 sites.

LAKE OZETTE: 4 mi. W of Clallam Bay on State 112, then 21 mi. S. Boundary of National Park. Campsites on lake accessible by walking across bridge from ranger station. Sites at Ericson Bay accessible by boat. Privately operated campground at resort is accessible by car. Boating, fishing, swimming, hiking. Ocean beach nearby (3-mi. trail).

LAKE OZETTE

LAKE SYLVIA STATE PARK: 10 mi. E of Aberdeen on US 101, then 1 mi. N. Small lake in hilly, forested setting. Cooking shelter with stoves, showers, swimming (lifeguard in summer), playground, fishing, hiking. 40 sites.

LENA CREEK: 14 mi. N of Hoodsport on US 101 then 9 mi. W. National Forest. Wooded river flat. Fishing, base of trail to Lena Lakes. 36 sites to be rebuilt; not recommended for trailers.

LEYENDECKER COUNTY PARK: 2 mi. N of Forks on US 101, then 9 mi. W on Rialto Beach road. Banks of river near junction of Soleduck and Bogachiel rivers. 6 sites.

LOWER HOH: Off US 101, 2 mi. S of bridge across Hoh River. State Department of Natural Resources land. Rain forest, on the river. Fishing. 10 sites; minimum development.

MERRILL-RING (Pillar Point): 38 mi. W of Port Angeles via State 112. Merrill-Ring company land with county operation. Fishing, crabbing. 30 sites; cooking shelter; trailer hookups.

MILLERSYLVANIA STATE PARK: 10 mi. S of Olympia slightly E of US 99 freeway. On shores of Deep Lake; forested. Cooking shelters (some with gas stoves), hot showers, playground, boating, fishing in lake which is heavily stocked. 231 sites.

MINNIE PETERSON: 3 mi. E of US 101 on Upper Hoh road. State Department of Natural Resources land. Rain forest setting including large spruce. Fishing. 6 sites.

MORA: 2 mi. N of Forks on US 101, then 12 mi. W on Rialto Beach road. National Park. Rain forest along the Quillayute River; swamp nearby. Site of one of first trading posts on Peninsula. One mile from the beach. Campfire programs and ranger-naturalist walks in summer, river fishing, smelting at nearby beach. 100 sites.

MORGANS CROSSING: 8 mi. E of US 101 on Upper Hoh Road. State Department of Natural Resources land. Rain forest riverbank. Fishing, 6 sites; minimum development.

MUKKAW BAY: 5½ mi. SW of Neah Bay. Makah Indian Reservation. Along the beach dunes. No facilities. Check with Tribal Council for current status.

NORTH FORK: 46 mi. N of Hoquiam on US 101, then 18 mi. E on north side of Lake Quinault. National Park. Forested stream-bank setting. Fishing, hiking. 10 sites; trailers not recommended.

OCEAN CITY STATE PARK: 20 mi. W of Hoquiam on State 109, then 1 mi. S. Open, flat land back from beach. Ocean swimming, surf fishing, razor clam digging. 182 sites; trailer hookups.

OIL CITY: 12 mi. W of US 101, S of Forks at end of Lower Hoh road. National Park. Forested riverbank; ocean adjacent. Undeveloped.

OLALLIE: 1 mi. E along S shore of Lake Quinault. National Forest. Forested lakeshore; nature trail nearby; boat launching. Fishing subject to Quinaielt Indian tribal regulation; special license; inquire locally. 13 sites; cooking shelter. Not recommended for trailers.

OLD FORT TOWNSEND STATE PARK: 2½ mi. S of Port Townsend on State 113. Site of early Army post. Hillside sloping down to bay; rhododendrons. Cooking shelter with gas stoves. Salt-water swimming, fishing, boating, clam digging. 28 campsites.

OLYMPIC HOT SPRINGS: 9 mi W. of Port Angeles on US 101, then 12 mi. S on Elwha road; last part steep and curving. National Park. Forested hillside. Fishing, hiking. 50 sites; not recommended for large trailers. Elevation 2,060 ft.

PENROSE POINT STATE PARK: 8 mi. S of State 3 at Key Center, west of Narrows Bridge. Cooking shelters, boating, salt-water fishing, clamming, swimming. 95 sites.

POTLATCH STATE PARK: 3½ mi. S of Hoodsport on US 101. Open grassy flat beside Hood Canal. Swimming, clams, oysters, salmon, 33 sites; trailer hookups.

PROMISED LAND: 28 mi. N Hoquiam US 101. Rayonier land. Situated on Stevens Creek. Cooking shelter, steam locomotive on display, children's wading beach, stream fishing. 20 sites.

QUEETS: 7 mi. S of US 101 bridge across Queets, then 13½ mi. E. National Park. Valley bottom, rain forest. River fishing, hiking. 12 sites; not recommended for trailers.

QUINAIELT INDIAN RESERVATION: Beach campground S of Taholah. Shaded. Operated by Tribal Council.

QUINAULT RIVER: 42 mi. N of Hoquiam on US 101, then 14 mi. E upriver. National Forest. Rain forest setting. Fishing, hiking. Being developed; 25 sites planned.

RAINBOW: 5 mi. S of Quilcene on US 101. National Forest. Cooking shelter, trail into canyon, fishing, scenic drive nearby. 12 sites.

SALT CREEK COUNTY PARK (Tongue Point): 12 mi. W of Port Angeles on State 112, then 4 mi. N. On bluff above Strait; marine view. Abandoned World War II bunkers. Cooking shelter, ball field, rifle range (open only in fall), beach access. 20 sites.

SCHAFER STATE PARK: 14 mi. E of Aberdeen on US 410, then 8 mi. N along Satsop. Grassy, forested river bottom. Cooking shelters, hot showers, community building with fireplace, swings, trout and steelhead fishing, hiking. 57 sites.

SEAL ROCK: 11 mi. S of Quilcene, just off US 101. National Forest. Forested hillside; gravel beach. Oysters. 42 sites.

SEKIU RIVER: 7 mi. W of Clallam Bay at mouth of Sekiu, just off State 112. Crown Zellerbach land. Forested, level ground along Strait. Fishing. Minimum development.

SEQUIM BAY STATE PARK: 4 mi. S of Sequim on US 101. Wooded hillside sloping to bay; both seclusion and recreation. Cooking shelters (including coin-operated stoves), showers, laundry, playground, ball field, salt-water swimming (lifeguard present in summer), boating, fishing, clamming. 107 sites; trailer hookups.

SHIP WRECK POINT: 11 mi. W of Sekiu off State 112. State Department of Natural Resources land. Flat point on Strait; young trees, grass, gravel beach. 3 sites; minimum development.

SLAB CAMP: 9 mi. W of Sequim on US 101, then 8 mi. S on county road. Forested. Fishing. 6 sites; minimum development. Trailers not recommended.

SPRUCE CREEK: 11 mi. E of US 101 on Upper Hoh Road. State Department of Natural Resources land. River bar; forested. Fishing. 5 sites; minimum development.

SOLEDUCK: 30 mi. W of Port Angeles on US 101, then 13 mi. S on Soleduck River road. National Park. Forest and river setting. Campfire programs in summer, hiking, fishing; swimming at resort nearby. 100 sites; not recommended for large trailers. Elevation 1,680.

SPENCER CREEK: 7 mi. S of Quilcene, W off US 101. Crown Zellerbach land. Forested hillside, secluded. Stream fishing. 12 sites.

SQUARE LAKE: S of Bremerton, 3 mi. W of State 16. State Department of Natural Resources land. Fishing, duck hunting. Cleared land; undeveloped.

STAIRCASE: 16 mi. W of Hoodsport beyond Lake Cushman. National Park. Forested; on Skokomish River. Hiking, river fishing. 60 sites; not recommended for large trailers.

STEELHEAD: 10 mi. S of Quilcene on US 101, then 12 mi. W up the Dosewallips. National Forest. Forested riverside. Fishing. Being developed; 10 sites planned.

SWINGING BRIDGE: 12 mi. E of Aberdeen on US 410, then 10 mi. N along west fork of Satsop. Weyerhaeuser Timber Co. land. Cooking shelter, playground, river "swimming hole," rustic bridge, fishing. 15 sites.

TUMBLING RAPIDS: 45 mi. W of Port Angeles on US 101; 12 mi. NE of Forks. Rayonier land. Forest and river setting. Cooking shelter, fishing. 20 sites.

TWANOH STATE PARK: 21 mi. SW of Bremerton on State 106. Shores of Hood Canal; shaded and grassy. Cooking shelters (including some coin-operated stoves), boating, swimming (lifeguard in summer), children's wading pool, playground, tennis courts, clamming, salt-water fishing, loop trail with hilltop views of Hood Canal and the Olympics. 91 sites; trailer hookups.

TWIN HARBORS STATE PARK: 21 mi. SW of Aberdeen near Westport on State 105. In trees behind dunes. Cooking shelters with lights and gas stoves, playground, deep-sea fishing, also surf and pier fishing, crabbing, clamming, driving on beach. 429 sites; trailer hookups.

WHITMAN COVE: 10 mi. S of State 3 at Key Center, west of Narrows Bridge. State Department of Natural Resources land. Mile-long beach. State Fisheries salmon-rearing pond, clam digging, oyster picking. 12 sites being developed.

WILLABY CREEK: 2 mi. E along S shore of Lake Quinault. National Forest. Forested lakeshore; boat launching. Fishing subject to Quinaielt Indian tribal regulation; special license; inquire locally. 18 sites.

WILLOUGHBY CREEK: 4 mi. E of US 101 on Upper Hoh road. State Department of Natural Resources land. Grassy clearing near river. 5 sites, minimum development.

WYNOCHEE FALLS: 9 mi. E of Aberdeen on US 410, then 42 mi. N along Wynoochee River. National Forest. Situated on riverbank. Fishing. 10 sites; large trailers not recommended.

FISHING

More than nine hundred lakes large enough to have names dot the Peninsula, plus uncounted small lakes and ephemeral ponds. Eight hundred miles of trout streams lace the valleys and two dozen rivers have winter steelhead runs. Salmon fishing is year-round sport. Surf fishing and smelting are popular in summer along the ocean beaches. Dock fishing is permitted on many municipal docks.

Tackle, boats—and advice—are readily available in all Peninsula cities and most crossroads communities.

BOY FISHING

Fresh water

Lowland Streams and Rivers: Cutthroat, Dolly Varden, rainbow, steelhead (searun rainbow or cutthroat), whitefish, five species of salmon (mostly kings and silvers), occasionally sturgeon.

Lowland Lakes: Brook trout, cutthroat, whitefish, silver trout (landlocked salmon), rainbow trout.

High-Country Streams: Rainbow, brook trout, whitefish a few places, cutthroat in upper Dosewallips.

High-Country Lakes: Brook trout, rainbow.

License:
State license on all waters except Olympic National Park where no license is required. Special license for Lake Quinault and all Quinaielt Indian Reservation land. Special punchcard for steelhead.

Seasons:
Streams: Mid-May to October.
Lowland Lakes: Late April to October.
High-Country Lakes: Late May to October.
Winter Steelhead: December to March (varies, depending on the river).
Limits:
Trout: 12 fish not to exceed 6 pounds, plus 1 fish.
Steelhead: 2 fish (check for current information).

Salt water

King Salmon (also called tyee, black, Chinook, spring, or blackmouth): Average weight 20-30 pounds; record 126 pound.

Silver Salmon (also called Coho or hooknose): Average weight 5-15 pounds; record 31 pounds.

Sockeye Salmon (also called red, blueback, Kokanee, or silver trout when landlocked): Average weight 5-15 pounds.

Humpback Salmon (also called pink): Average weight 5-15 pounds.

Dog Salmon (also called chum or calico): Average weight 5-15 pounds.

Ling Cod: up to 4 feet long, weighing 40 pounds; also some black cod, red cod, and bull cod.

Rockfish: Rock cod averaging a few pounds each, red snapper, and ocean perch.

Flatfish: Halibut up to 100 pounds, sole, flounders, and sand dabs.

Smelt and herring.

License:
None required for salt-water sport fishing.
Season:
Open all year.
Major salmon runs: King: April to July, also August to October. Silver: September to January. Sockeye: July to December. Humpback: August to September. Dog: October to January.

Charter Boats:
Olympia, Shelton, Bremerton, Port Angeles, Sekiu, Neah Bay, LaPush, Aberdeen-Hoquiam, Ocean Shores, Westport.

CLAMS, OYSTERS, CRABS

Low tide is the time for clamming, oyster picking, or crabbing—the lower, the better. Tide tables are published in Peninsula newspapers and are available at sporting goods stores and most Olympic National Park ranger stations.

There are state shellfish research laboratories at Aberdeen and at Whitney Point, near Quilcene.

Razor Clams

Digging: Look for a "dimple" in the sand at low tide; then dig with the shovel on the seaward side and the blade pointing straight down. The clam will be down 8 to 12 inches and digging fast to escape. Reach in by hand.

Preparing: Shells are thin and easily opened. Remove dark digestive organs. Fry meat, or use in chowder.

Public Razor Clam Beaches:

Kalaloch: on US 101 S of Forks.

Ocean Shores, Oyehut, Ocean City, Copalis Beach, Roosevelt Beach, Ocean Grove, Pacific Beach, Sunset Beach, Moclips: W of Aberdeen-Hoquiam along State 109.

Twin Harbors: State 109 near Westport.

Permissible on any public beach; no license or other permit required.

Season: March to mid-October; after mid-October on week ends and holidays only.

Limit: 18 clams, any size (all clams dug must be kept and counted part of the limit); limit is subject to change on recommendation by State shellfish biologists.

Hardshell Clams

Digging: Dig on rocky beaches with a shovel or pitchfork, then feel with the hands; often hands alone suffice, no shovel. Clams are 2 to 10 inches down and do not dig to escape as razor clams do. Some show their location by "squirting," some do not. Fill in holes after digging because mounded sand may kill clams by making it impossible for their siphons to reach the surface to feed.

Goeducks are usually 2 to 4 feet down. A special open-ended "goeduck can" or a length of oversize stovepipe pressed down around the clam helps keep sand and water from caving in the hole while digging is in progress. Goeducks weigh 2 to 4 pounds each. The name comes from the Indian *goe-tuck*, meaning "master clam." Horse clams are close to the same size and also are edible, particularly in chowder.

Preparing: Wash and put in a covered pot without adding water. Steam just until the shells open (overcooking toughens). Dip in butter and eat from the shell, or use in chowder. Goeduck steaks can be fried.

Public Clam Beaches:

Penrose State Park: Off State 3 S of Bremerton.

Whitman's Cove: S of Home, which is off State 3 S of Bremerton.

Kopachuck State Park: Off State 3 S of Bremerton.

Harper County Park: State 160 E of Bremerton.

Illahee State Park: N of Bremerton off State 303.

Fay Bainbridge State Park: N end Bainbridge Island.

Belfair State Park: State 300 S of Bremerton.

Kitsap Memorial Park: Near E end of Hood Canal Bridge.

Lilliwaup: 2 beaches on US 101 just N of Lilliwaup.

Dosewallips State Park: US 101 S of Brinnon.

Dabob Bay: Pt. Whitney road SE of Quilcene.

Oak Head: Tip of Toandos Peninsula SE of Quilcene.

Shine: Off State 104 near W end of Hood Canal Bridge.

Oak Bay: Off State 9 S of Hadlock.

Sequim Bay State Park: US 101 SE of Sequim.

Jamestown: N of Sequim.

Dungeness: N of Sequim.

Oysters

Picking: Oysters are exposed at low tide and need only to be picked up. If possible shuck them at the beach and leave the shells for oyster larvae to attach to.

Preparing: Open by inserting knife and cutting abductor muscle. Eat raw, fried, broiled, in stew, or baked in the shell over campfire coals.

Season: Open all year. No license required.

Limit: 36 whole oysters or 4 pints of shelled meat.

Public Oyster Beaches:

Whitman's Cove: S of Home, which is off State 3 S of Bremerton.

Belfair State Park: State 300 S of Bremerton.

Twanoh State Park: State 106 SW of Bremerton.

Potlatch State Park: US 101 N of Shelton.

Lilliwaup: 2 beaches on US 101 just N of Lilliwaup.

Dosewallips State Park: US 101 S of Brinnon.

Seal Rock Forest Camp: Off US 101 N of Brinnon.

Dabob Bay: Pt. Whitney off US 101 S of Quilcene.

Oak Head: Tip of Toandos Peninsula SE of Quilcene.

Shine: Off State 104 S of Pt. Ludlow.

Grays Harbor: N side off State 109.

Crabs

Catching: Rake through eelgrass with a garden rake or pitchfork until the tines strike what feels like a rock; or gently probe in tidepools or low tide channels. Lift the crab by scooping under it. Tines should be padded (adhesive tape or short lengths of rubber tubing). It is unlawful to pierce the shell. Crabs may not be taken by spearing, trawling, seining, or gill netting. Minus tides are best. Hip boots or a wet suit are advisable in winter.

Preparing: Boil 20 minutes, then lift off back and clean. Crack shell of legs and abdomen to remove meat. Eat with sauce, in salad, or in casseroles.

Season: Open all year for sport crabbing. No license required.

Limit: 6 males, at least 6¼ inches across the back. Females and softshell crabs (moulting stage) may not be taken. Sexes are easily distinguished by the movable plate on the underside of the abdomen. It is much longer than broad in the male; almost as broad as long in the female.

Public Crab Beaches: Dungeness, on the Strait east of Port Angeles, is best known; also Pillar Point W of Port Angeles, North Jetty and lagoons of Grays Harbor, and occasionally along ocean beaches. Make local inquiry. Crabbing varies from year to year.

Other Edible Seafood

Octopus: Boil, bake, or pound the meat and fry quickly.
Squid: Boil, bake, or pound the meat and fry quickly.
Native Abalone (not red abalone): Pound the meat and fry quickly.
Sea cucumber (rollops): Peel off skin; pound meat and fry.
Sea urchins: Eat raw; best when orange-colored.
Gooseneck barnacles: Use in chowder.
Piddock clams: Use in chowder.
Mussels: Use in chowder.

HUNTING

Most of the lowlands of the Peninsula are open to hunting, including state and federal land and commercial tree farms; Olympic National Park and the offshore national wildlife refuges are sanctuaries closed to hunting. Elk, deer, ducks, and geese are the main game species, but for something out of the ordinary try for bear or cougar. Inquire locally for current details.

Seasons

Game Birds: Mid-September to late November for blue grouse, chukkar, and Hungarian partridge. Mid-October to December for band-tail pigeon, snipe, and quail.

Waterfowl: Mid-October to late December for ducks and geese. December to January for brant.

Game Animals: Deer season opens in mid-October; elk season in early November. Snowshoe rabbits from mid-October to March.

Predators: Year-round season on bear, cougar, coyote, and fox. (Subject to change; check current status.)

License

State license is required of all hunters regardless of age; for ducks and geese a federal migratory bird stamp is also required of persons over sixteen years.

Main Public Hunting Areas

Olympic National Forest; Olympic Game Range (north of Aberdeen); State Department of Natural Resources land; tree farms, subject to permission and restrictions of owners (maps and information available each fall at tree farm foresters' offices).

WEATHER

Weather on the Olympic Peninsula is mild the year round, warmed in winter by the Japanese Current and protected in summer by the Cascade Mountains from the heat of eastern Washington. Winter temperatures seldom dip below freezing, and summer maximums are typically in the 70's. On Tatoosh Island, off Cape Flattery, the growing season is 306 days per year—two weeks longer than at New Orleans and more than twice as long as at Bar Harbor, Maine, even though the latitude here is more northerly than at Nova Scotia.

Rain can fall hard and fast, raising rivers as much as six feet in a day; but usually it is gentle. Records for the town of Forks show no month without rain in thirty years, although summer months average only about two inches and have dropped as low as .31 inch. At Wynoochee Oxbow, north of Aberdeen, 54 inches of rain once fell in a single month. In the rain forest, mean precipitation is from 120 to 140 inches per year; yet fifty miles away at Sequim, on the north tip of the Peninsula, it averages just over one-tenth that amount.

From a traveler's standpoint mid-June through October is usually the best season. Days generally are warm, although sweaters are needed in the evening. Winters, while not cold, incline to be overcast and spring is rainy. Frequently, and at any time of year, a day that is cloudy along Hood Canal will be clear along the Pacific Coast—and vice versa. Or at Hurricane Ridge, hikers will be basking in sunshine while salmon fishermen huddle in rain slickers along the Strait. Information on current weather at various points on the Peninsula is usually available at National Park Service headquarters in Port Angeles.

SOURCES OF INFORMATION

The availability of supplies and services, the condition of roads and trails, the schedule of events, vary from year to year. For current information check with the appropriate agency.

Chambers of Commerce (all types of tourist information):

Aberdeen	Port Angeles
Bremerton	Port Townsend
Forks	Sequim
Hoquiam	Shelton
Olympia	

Olympic Peninsula Resort and Hotel Association (accommodations):
c/o Washington State Ferries, Colman Terminal, Seattle, Washington 98104

Washington State Ferries (schedules and fares):
Colman Ferry Terminal, Seattle, Washington 98104

Olympic National Park (schedule of events; lists of accommodations and services, fire permits):
Headquarters: 600 Park Avenue, Port Angeles, Washington 98362
Ranger Stations (year around):

Elwha	Kalaloch
Heart O' the Hills	Lake Crescent
Hoh Rain Forest	Lake Quinault
Mora	Staircase

Summer Ranger Stations:

Deer Park	Queets
Dosewallips	Quinault (East Fork)
Lake Ozette	Soleduck

Olympic National Forest (maps; road conditions):
Main Office: Post Office Bldg., Olympia, Washington 98501
District Ranger Stations:

Forks	Quilcene
Hoodsport	Quinault
Shelton	

State Department of Natural Resources (campsite information; fire permits):
Main Office: Public Lands Bldg., Olympia, Washington 98501
District Offices:

Forks	Port Angeles
Montesano	Port Orchard
Shelton	

State Parks and Recreation Commission (facilities in Parks):
Main Office: 522 South Franklin, Olympia, Washington 98501

State Department of Game (hunting regulations):
Main Office: 600 North Capitol Way, Olympia, Washington 98501
Game Protectors:

Aberdeen	Forks
Bremerton	Olympia
Chimacum	Port Angeles
Elma	Shelton

State Department of Fisheries (fish and shellfish information):
General Administration Building, Olympia, Washington 98501

State Highways Commission:
Main Office: Highways Building, Olympia, Washington 98501

U.S. Fish and Wildlife Service (National Wildlife Refuges, information and permits):
Willapa National Wildlife Refuge, Ilwaco, Washington 98624

Bureau of Indian Affairs:
Western Washington Agency, 1620 Hewitt Avenue, Everett, Washington 98201

UNUSUAL FLORA AND FAUNA

Aspects of the Olympic Peninsula that are of particular significance biologically include certain plant species that grow here but nowhere else, a marmot generally considered a distinct sub-species exclusive to the Olympics, and conversely several mammals never native here but common in the Cascade Range.

Also, trees of eight different species believed to be the largest individuals of their kind in the world have been credited to the Peninsula, five of them in the rain forest. Such lists, however, constantly change as remote areas are explored in detail and new "records" discovered—matters of human interest but of less significance biologically than the underlying fact that an unusual number of tree species on the Peninsula reach unusually great size in a small geographical area.

Endemic Plant Species

Astragulus cottoni; locoweed.
Campanula piperi; Piper bellflower.
Erigeron flettii; fleabane.
Erysimum arenicola; wallflower.
Senecio websteri; senecio.
Petrophytum hendersoni; hardhack.
Viola flettii; Flett violet.

Record-Size Trees

Abies anabilis; Pacific silver fir. Diameter 6'10"; height 186'.
Abies lasiocarpa; subalpine fir. Diameter 6'8½"; height 129'.
Alnus rubra; red alder. Diameter 3'9"; height 89'.
Chamaecyperis nootkatensis; Alaska-cedar. Diameter 7'8"; height 114'.
Picea sitchensis; Sitka spruce. Diameter 13'3"; height 214'.
Pseudostuga menziesii; Douglas-fir. Diameter 14'5½"; height 221'.
Thuja plicata; Western redcedar. Diameter 21'; height 130'.
Tsuga heterophylla; Western hemlock. Diameter 8'7"; height 125'.

"Missing" Mammal Species

Erethizon dorsatum; porcupine.
Gulo luscus; wolverine.
Lynx canadensis lynx.
Microtus richardsoni; water vole.
Ochotona princeps; pika.
Oreamnos americanus; mountain goat.
Ovis canadensis; mountain sheep.
Spermophilus saturatus; Cascade golden-mantled ground squirrel.
Synaptomys borealis; Northern bog lemming.
Ursus chelan grizzly bear.
Vulpes fulva; red fox.

Endemic Mammal

Marmota olympus; Olympic marmot.

READING LIST

ANDREWS, RALPH. *Indian Primitive.* Seattle: Superior Publishing Co., 1960. Early-day Indian life presented by historic Northwest photographs; conveys feeling of Peninsula Indians although not particularized to them.

BINNS, ARCHIE. *Sea in the Forest.* New York: Doubleday & Co., 1953. Historical account including exploration, settlement, and early logging.

CAHALANE, VICTOR H. *Meeting the Mammals.* New York: Macmillan & Co., 1943. Informative and highly readable popular discussions of U.S. mammals, including major Olympic species.

DANNER, WILBERT R. *Geology of Olympic National Park.* Seattle: University of Washington Press, 1955. Detailed account, popularly written.

HULT, RUBY EL. *Untamed Olympics.* Portland, Ore.: Binfords & Mort, 1954. Anecdotal history of settlement and early development.

KIRK, RUTH with photographs by Johsel Namkung and the author. *The Olympic Rain Forest.* Seattle: University of Washington Press, 1966. Large format presentation of the rain forest in words and pictures, including color.

KIRK, RUTH. *The Olympic Seashore.* Port Angeles, Wash.: Olympic Natural History Association, 1962. History and natural history of Peninsula's west coast with emphasis on where to go.

KITCHIN, EDWARD A. *Birds of the Olympic Peninsula.* Port Angeles, Wash.: Olympic Stationers, 1949. 261 species found on the Peninsula; drawings.

LEISSLER, FREDERICK. *Roads and Trails of Olympic National Park.* Seattle: University of Washington Press, 1957. Detailed logs of mileage to points of interest within the Park; brief descriptions.

LYONS, CHESTER P. *Trees, Shrubs, and Flowers to Know in Washington.* Vancouver, Canada: J. M. Dent, 1956. Most comprehensive, easy-to-use guide to plants.

MORGAN, MURRAY. *The Last Wilderness.* New York: The Viking Press, 1956. Enjoyable account of Peninsula history from Indians to present.

MOSER, DON. *The Peninsula.* San Francisco: Sierra Club, 1962. Brief text describing Peninsula; lavish photographs.

SHARPE, GRANT, and WENONAH. *101 Wildflowers of Olympic National Park.* Seattle: University of Washington Press, 1954. Guide to identification of most common flowers, especially alpine.

UNDERHILL, RUTH. *Indians of the Pacific Northwest.* Lawrence, Kansas: Haskell Institute, 1944. Basic account of Northwest Indians; out of print.

WOOD, ROBERT. *Across the Olympic Mountains.* Seattle: University of Washington Press, 1967. Lively historical account.

ANDERSON PASS
SHELTER
O'NEIL CREEK
SHELTER
HART LAKE 12.8
10.8 QUINAULT ROAD
DOSEWALL
ROAD 15.5

INDEX

Entries given in italics refer to illustrations.

THE AUTHOR

CAMPGROUNDS

1. Twin Harbors State Park
2. Ocean City State Park
3. Promised Land
4. Quinaielt Indian Reservation
5. Willaby Creek
6. Olallie
7. Falls Creek
8. July Creek
9. Quinault River
10. Campbell Tree Grove
11. North Fork
12. Graves Creek
13. Kings Bottom
14. Queets
15. Kalaloch
16. Copper Mine Bottom
17. Oil City
18. Lower Hoh
19. Minnie Peterson
20. Willoughby Creek
21. Morgans Crossing
22. Spruce Creek
23. Huelsdonk Bridge
22. Hoh
25. Bogachiel State Park
26. Leyendecker County Park
27. Mora
28. Kiahanie Forest Camp
29. Tumbling Rapids
30. Lake Ozette (also Ericson Bay)
31. Mukkaw Bay
32. Ship Wreck Point
33. Sekiu River
34. Clallam River
35. Merrill-Ring (Pillar Point)
36. Deep Creek
37. Klahowya
38. Fairholm
39. Sol Duc
40. Olympic Hot Springs
41. Altaire
42. Elwha
43. Salt Creek County Park (Tongue Point)
44. Heart O' the Hills
45. Deer Park
46. Slab Camp
47. Dungeness Forks
48. East Crossing
49. Dungeness Bay and State Park
50. Sequim Bay State Park
51. Old Fort Townsend State Park
52. Fort Flagler State Park
53. Kitsap Memorial State Park
54. Falls View
55. Big Quil River
56. Rainbow
57. Spencer Creek
58. Seal Rock
59. Dosewallips State Park
60. Steelhead
61. Dosewallips (National Park)
62. Elkhorn Forest Camp
63. Collins
64. Hamma Hamma
65. Lena Creek
66. Fossen Lake
67. Bob Camp
68. Osborne Lake
69. Lake Cushman State Park
70. Big Creek
71. Staircase
72. Brown Creek
73. Potlatch State Park
74. Twanoh State Park
75. Aldrich Lake
76. Haven Lake County Park
77. Camp Rickey
78. Camp Spillman
79. Belfair State Park
80. Camp Correll
81. Green Mountain
82. Illahee State Park
83. Fay Bainbridge State Park
84. Square Lake
85. Kopachuck State Park
86. Penrose Point State Park
87. Whitman Cove
88. Millersylvania State Park
89. Schafer State Park
90. Swinging Bridge
91. Lake Sylvia State Park
92. Wynoochee Falls

PICNIC AREAS

1. Lake Aberdeen Park
2. Lions City Park
3. Rialto Beach
4. Forks City Park
5. North Point
6. La Poel
7. Lake Crescent Roadside Picnic Tables
8. Lincoln City Park
9. Ediz Hook
10. Hurricane Ridge
11. Waterhole
12. Port Williams
13. Discovery Bay Roadside Rest Area
14. Chetzemoka City Park
15. East Beach County Park
16. Oak Bay County Park
17. Chimacum County Park
18. Hicks County Park
19. East Quilcene Roadside Rest Area
20. Quilcene County Park
21. Mt. Walker Summit
22. Roadside Rest Area
23. Roadside Rest Area
24. Roadside Rest Area
25. Purdy Canyon
26. Shelton Roadside Park
27. Nahwatzel Lake
28. Agate Peninsula County Park
29. Walker County Park
30. Kingston County Park
31. Evergreen City Park
32. Fort Ward State Park
33. Harper County Park
34. Point Robinson County Park
35. Gig Harbor City Park
36. Priest Point City Park
37. Tumwater Falls
38. County Line Roadside Rest Area